Unintended Consequences and the Social Sciences

NEW THINKING IN POLITICAL ECONOMY

Series Editor: Peter J. Boettke, *George Mason University, USA*

New Thinking in Political Economy aims to encourage scholarship in the intersection of the disciplines of politics, philosophy and economics. It has the ambitious purpose of reinvigorating political economy as a progressive force for understanding social and economic change.

The series is an important forum for the publication of new work analysing the social world from a multidisciplinary perspective. With increased specialization (and professionalization) within universities, interdisciplinary work has become increasingly uncommon. Indeed, during the 20th century, the process of disciplinary specialization reduced the intersection between economics, philosophy and politics and impoverished our understanding of society. Modern economics in particular has become increasingly mathematical and largely ignores the role of institutions and the contribution of moral philosophy and politics.

New Thinking in Political Economy will stimulate new work that combines technical knowledge provided by the 'dismal science' and the wisdom gleaned from the serious study of the 'worldly philosophy'. The series will reinvigorate our understanding of the social world by encouraging a multidisciplinary approach to the challenges confronting society in the new century.

For a full list of Edward Elgar published titles, including the titles in this series, visit our website at www.e-elgar.com.

Unintended Consequences and the Social Sciences
An Intellectual History

Lorenzo Infantino

Professor of Philosophy of Social Sciences, LUISS Guido Carli, Rome, Italy

NEW THINKING IN POLITICAL ECONOMY

Cheltenham, UK • Northampton, MA, USA

© Lorenzo Infantino 2023

All rights reserved. No part of this publication may be reproduced, stored in a retrieval system or transmitted in any form or by any means, electronic, mechanical or photocopying, recording, or otherwise without the prior permission of the publisher.

Published by
Edward Elgar Publishing Limited
The Lypiatts
15 Lansdown Road
Cheltenham
Glos GL50 2JA
UK

Edward Elgar Publishing, Inc.
William Pratt House
9 Dewey Court
Northampton
Massachusetts 01060
USA

A catalogue record for this book
is available from the British Library

Library of Congress Control Number: 2023939820

This book is available electronically in the Elgaronline
Economics subject collection
http://dx.doi.org/10.4337/9781035318049

Printed on elemental chlorine free (ECF)
recycled paper containing 30% Post-Consumer Waste

ISBN 978 1 0353 1803 2 (cased)
ISBN 978 1 0353 1804 9 (eBook)

Printed and bound in the USA

To José Antonio de Aguirre and Raimondo Cubeddu, tireless scholars and dearest friends

Contents

Preface		ix
1	The problem of the unintended consequences of human actions	1
	1.1 Unintended consequences, religion and magic	1
	1.2 Unintended consequences and polytheism	2
	1.3 The "government of men" (and of the gods) and the "government of the law"	6
	1.4 Plato and the new intentional order	7
	1.5 Unintended consequences as the object of the social sciences	10
2	Pierre Bayle and Bernard de Mandeville	19
	2.1 True individualism and false individualism	19
	2.2 Bayle: limits of knowledge, religion and motives for action	21
	2.3 Mandeville: from human fallibility to unintended order	24
	2.4 Mercantilists or liberals?	28
3	Francis Hutcheson and David Hume	38
	3.1 Between past and future	38
	3.2 Hutcheson on the shoulders of Shaftesbury	39
	3.3 Hume betrayed by Hutcheson	42
	3.4 Hume and unintended order	45
	3.5 Research traditions	48
	3.6 Appendix: Josiah Tucker	50
4	Charles-Louis de Montesquieu and Adam Smith	57
	4.1 Montesquieu and the variability of models of life	57
	4.2 Montesquieu between the myth of Sparta and the Great Society	60
	4.3 Smith and the birth of social norms	63
	4.4 Smith: division of labour and "rule of law"	66
	4.5 Appendix: Adam Ferguson	69

5	Initial continuities and discontinuities	78
	5.1 Immediate Scottish influences in political theory: Edmund Burke and Benjamin Constant	78
	5.2 Inside economic theory: utilitarian in the broad sense and utilitarian in the narrow sense	82
	5.3 Inside sociology: the discontinuity of Auguste Comte and the continuity of Herbert Spencer	86
	5.4 Appendix: Spencer and Darwin	90
6	Additional considerations	99
References		105
Index		116

Preface

> I have hitherto sometimes spoken as if the variations [...] had been due to chance. This, of course, is a wholly incorrect expression, but it serves to acknowledge plainly our ignorance of the cause of each particular variation. (Charles Darwin)

When reference is made to the social sciences, it almost seems that they do not have their own object and that everything remains confined within vague (and perhaps vain) debates on the various issues of collective life. There was, however, a period in history, which was given the name of the "age of society".[1] It was an historical turning point at which there occurred what others had no hesitation in calling "the discovery of society".[2] At that time, the compartmentalization of today did not exist. The reader will know that scholars such as Bernard de Mandeville, David Hume, Charles-Louis de Montesquieu and Adam Smith marshalled their knowledge of the entire territory of social phenomena. They were aware that human beings live in a state of ignorance and fallibility; and they well understood that every action must measure itself against a scarcity of resources and time.

Those thinkers set themselves the task of emancipating us from the dominant belief throughout the history of humanity, which held that social events are the direct consequence of the will of an actor of some kind: a conviction that leads to attributing what cannot be ascribed to human action to the intervention of other entities. Phenomena that are not the immediate outcome of the intentionality of human beings (and which are nevertheless determined by their actions) are thus transformed into a product of the will of a population of invisible forces which, either evoked or on their own initiative, participate, for better or for worse, in the events of everyday life. Unintended consequences disappear. There exists an order which is intentionally established or, as Max Weber vividly wrote, one lives in a situation "saturated with order".[3]

Therefore, the "discovery of society" took place when people stopped seeing behind every social phenomenon the action of the direct human and/or divine will of someone. This left a void that was filled by resorting to the intersubjective relationship, which possesses, as it was emphasized, the ability to "secrete", "on its own and unescapably, language, habits, customs, laws and public power".[4] Everything revolved around the need to obtain the cooperation of others: what impels everyone to adapt their own actions to those of their neighbours. Thus, purposes for which it is not possible to obtain cooperation are eliminated; and the conditions to which the actors subject each other, that is to say social norms and institutions, are produced without any planning.

This was the idea which allowed us to turn our backs on the old conception and shed light on the events which occur in the social field. But shifting attention from the subject's motives to the consequences of their action was not an easy task. Mandeville left us many caustic pages on the rhetoric of good intentions. He was preceded by Pierre Bayle: his words were perhaps less provocative. And yet the writings of both were viewed with suspicion and disapproval. This is borne out by the hostility, more than the incomprehension, with which Francis Hutcheson targeted Bayle and, more openly, Mandeville, to which one can also add the way he treated Hume.

It was felt that the refusal to base social order on intentions (and their control by an invisible population, placed beyond proofs and refutations) would plunge collective life into irreversible chaos, and render it impossible for human actions to be made compatible with each other. This showed a failure to understand that the action of each must be judged by what it determines in the context inside which it is performed. The actors intentionally exchange means; this is certainly done to achieve their purposes. And yet, in such a way, each individual contributes unintentionally to the achievement of the other's goals.

As has been contended, this may lead to the statement that a "miracle of logic" is claimed to be accomplished.[5] It is not the case. If we subject cooperation, precisely because it is such, to a dual reading, every semblance of a "miracle" collapses: we can see that Ego pursues his goals through the means obtained from Alter and that Alter pursues his goals with the means obtained from Ego. Voluntary exchange brings each of us to cooperate unintentionally in the achievement of the aims of others. There is no need for a mandatory hierarchy of ends; and there is no need for a privileged source of knowledge to legitimize such a hierarchy: we are all ignorant and fallible. The order that is established is of an unintended type; it cannot be attributed to the will of anyone in particular. It has fuelled an ateleological social process. It is a continual exploration of the unknown, which grasps the unintended consequences of a positive character and which highlights those of a negative character and the errors that have produced them. This makes it possible to eliminate patterns of behaviour that do not respond, or no longer respond, to the expectations of the actors; and brings about the form of cultural selection that, as we shall see in the final part of the book, had so much influence on Herbert Spencer and Charles Darwin.

In other words, putting the consequences of an action in the place of intentions means that prescription gives way to choice.[6] The former is the instrument with which one makes a single hierarchy of ends mandatory and dictates the contents of each person's life. The latter, on the other hand, is the means which places everyone in a position to exercise their own autonomous decision-making. We are confronted by radically different ways of delimiting the boundaries between actions. The normative *habitat* changes. In the former case, what is "just" is imposed (and the individual has no autonomy); in the latter case, what is "unjust" is prevented (and the rest is left to the choice of the actor). It is an issue that Hume understood perfectly. This explains, even if his philosophy of law has been (and is) often neglected, his insistence on the need to replace the "government of men" (and/or divinities) with the "government of the law"; a need that did not escape Montesquieu and that was very clear to Smith, who wanted, as we know, to write a work on the theory of law, a project confirmed even at the time when the thread of his life was about to snap.

The authors on which I have mainly focused share the idea that the object of the social sciences should be the study of unintended consequences. As we know, Joseph A. Schumpeter called this approach "methodological individualism".[7] He also pointed out that "between economics and psychology there are *no* relations" in terms of object.[8] Despite this, the individualistic method has often been placed within the province of utilitarianism as inspired by Jeremy Bentham. In this way, two research traditions that should be kept separate have been combined. In cultural evolutionism, human action is the element that serves to explain the social process. In utilitarianism narrowly understood, there is no action; there is simply a "felicific calculus", carried out by a subject who has access to the *relevant data* and therefore escapes the uncertainty of interaction. Everything is reduced to an exercise in logic; and this can generate the illusion that everyone knows everything. But the fact is that the *relevant data* are not in the possession of any individual mind. No actor exists who can know in advance what others, also placed in an unwavering condition of ignorance and fallibility, decide to do.[9] No one can avoid the problem of unintended consequences.

Only an unforgivable misunderstanding could (and can) therefore induce anyone to put "methodological individualism" on the same level as utilitarianism in the narrow sense. Dugald Stewart and Carl Menger, both from the evolutionary tradition, can help us here. The former absorbed the entirety of the lesson of the Scottish Enlightenment; and recalled the need to achieve the "decomposition" of social phenomena through human action.[10] The latter authored one of the most important pages in the debate on the methodology of the social sciences; and he rightly spoke of the "compositive method", with which he meant that social facts are the product of the reciprocal and unplanned co-adaptation of individual plans.[11]

There remain no further preliminary points to make. I would just like to mention that this book has taken a long time to come to light. In the early 1980s, when it was still not possible to obtain books *on demand*, or to read remotely works one could not physically access, I spent so many days in the Bodleian Library at Oxford, collecting the material that I thought I would use to speedily draft this book. But things turned out differently. As happens to everyone, I had to change my plans. However, I did not abandon the goal, nor the thinkers on whom, even before that period, I was working and who have been, throughout all this time, among my permanent sources of learning. More precisely, I can say that the delay with which I deliver this book to the reader today has been of great benefit to me: because it has allowed me to let my initial ideas settle and to acquire new ones.

In addition to José Antonio de Aguirre and Raimondo Cubeddu, to whom this volume is dedicated, the first version of the text was read by Giovanni Boniolo; to all three I express my most heartfelt gratitude. Numerous other people have also given me their attention. I must at least mention: Pierpaolo Benigno, Enrico Colombatto, Emma Galli, Giampaolo Garzarelli, Marcello Messori, Salvatore Nisticò, Pietro Reichlin; to all of them I address my warm thanks, as well as to Simona Fallocco and Nicola Iannello, for their unfailing help and advice. None of the people mentioned above is in any way responsible for what is set out in the following pages.

Rome, LUISS Guido Carli, January 2022
L.I.

NOTES

1. See Schultz (1969), Mongardini (1970) and the bibliography referred therein.
2. Wolin (2006), pp. 273–276.
3. Weber (1924), p. 32.
4. I am here making use of expressions that were used by Ortega y Gasset ([1930] 1946–83g, p. 117) in attacking contractualism. As was explained by Simmel (1908, pp. 6–7), in whom Ortega found inspiration, it is necessary to explain social phenomena "on the basis of reciprocal action".
5. See Durkheim ([1893] 1964), p. 415.
6. Becker (1950), pp. 25–32; Germani (1975), pp. 25–32.
7. Schumpeter (1908), p. 90.
8. Op. cit., p. 144. See also Weber ([1922] 1978, vol. 1, pp. 19–22); Mises ([1933] 1981a, pp. 2 and 57).
9. Hayek (1949), p. 77.
10. Stewart (1829), p. 10.
11. The expression "compositive method" is from a handwritten annotation by Menger (see Hayek, 1979, p. 67, note 4).

1. The problem of the unintended consequences of human actions

> Hence all the fruitless industry to account for the ill appearances of nature [and life], and to save the honour of the gods; while we must acknowledge the reality of that evil and disorder, with which the world so much abounds. (David Hume)
>
> [...] in a world that was a part of an "ethical, cosmic order", in a world in which human powers were directed according to the needs of unification and harmony, the tragedy would not be possible. (Max Scheler)

1.1 UNINTENDED CONSEQUENCES, RELIGION AND MAGIC

From the earliest days of their long evolution, human beings have had to reckon with social phenomena deriving from their actions, but not attributable to their will. The belief that, behind each event, whether social or natural, there must always lie somebody's will led them to attribute every phenomenon not directly ascribable to their own actions to the intervention of an invisible population of spirits and divinities. Aristotle recalled that the magistrates who oversaw all public sacrifices were called "in one place archons, in another kings, and in a third prytanes".[1] And this prompted Fustel de Coulanges to argue that the three words (archon, king, *prytane*) had for a long time been "synonymous", so that "the personage to whom was applied indifferently one of these three names – perhaps all of them at the same time – was the priest of the city".[2] In turn, Herbert Spencer pointed out that in those kinds of societies "the secular and the sacred are but little distinguished".[3] And James G. Frazer affirmed that "the union of a royal title with priestly duties was common in ancient Italy and Greece".[4]

As Frazer himself specified, "kings were revered, in many cases not merely as priests, that is, as intercessors between man and god, but as themselves gods, able to bestow upon their subjects and worshipers those blessings which are commonly supposed to be beyond the reach of man".[5] And not only that. The king was "quite often" also a magician, who was asked to control events directly. This is why magic and religion were often "united" and rituals were at the same time magical and religious.[6] This, however, does not prevent us from bearing in mind the "radical conflict of principle" which opposes religion and magic.[7] The latter is a power "residing exclusively in man", which is activated

1

by the "magical art";[8] the magician has his own "haughty self-sufficiency", his own "demeanour" is "arrogant" towards the "higher powers", to whom he exhibits the "unabashed claim to exercise a sway like theirs".[9] Therefore, the magician operates on his own account; and what occurs is to be ascribed exclusively to his action. The situation is quite different in the religious field, where the priest is only the "medium", the "intercessor between god and man".[10]

In such a context, one can identify three distinct territories. The first is that of the profane, limited because the knowledge and technical skills of a human being are limited; the second is dominated by magic; the third pertains to religion. But all three territories are linked by the fact that what occurs is intentionally willed. The actors to whom the results are attributed are respectively a man, a magician, and a divinity or a plurality of divinities.[11] And yet, if we consider that magic and religion "open up escapes" from situations and impasses which offer no other way out,[12] we realize that recourse to them is generated by man's need to find help in achieving what he is unable to accomplish on his own. With an eye to the peoples of the Trobriand Islands, Bronislaw Malinowski wrote: "It is most significant that in the lagoon fishing, where man can rely completely upon his knowledge and skill, magic does not exist, while in the open-sea fishing, full of danger and uncertainty, there is extensive magical ritual to secure safety and good results."[13] And he added: "religious faith establishes, fixes and enhances all valuable mental attitudes, such as reverence for tradition, harmony with the environment, courage and confidence".[14]

This means that the intervention of magical and divine powers is evoked to prevent human beings from suffering unintended consequences of a negative kind and to allow them to benefit from unintended consequences of a positive kind.[15] Whatever the result ultimately achieved, what from the strictly profane point of view is an unintended outcome is thus transformed into an intended outcome, attributable to the will of the magician or of God. In other terms, what is beyond the control of the profane falls under the control of magic or religion.

1.2 UNINTENDED CONSEQUENCES AND POLYTHEISM

The idea of attributing everything that cannot be considered the intentional product of human action to the intervention of mysterious forces prevents us from understanding the reason lying behind the process which leads to the growth of our knowledge. As Karl R. Popper wrote, philosophical (and scientific) problems "are always rooted in urgent problems outside philosophy, and they die if these roots decay".[16] This suggests that, independently of whether they are generated by the relationship with nature or the relationship with one's fellows, unintended consequences are, exactly as Popper said, problems rooted in human life.[17] And yet, because this places their origin in a territory that lies beyond proofs and refutations, transforming them into the intentional product of cosmic forces precludes us from investigating the conditions which make them possible.

Restricting our attention exclusively to the social sphere, this transformation brings us to the belief that rules and institutions are a direct creation of some divine will, which manifests itself through its own representative, an "intermediary" between God and man. Thus is born the myth of the Great Legislator, who is given the task of dictating the contents of each person's life and the ways in which such contents must be realized. The social order, that is to say the compatibility of actions, is imposed by the holder or holders of a monopoly of communication with the cosmic forces and a consequent monopoly of authoritative roles.

The complete acceptance of this conception goes hand in hand with permanent control of the actors' intentions. For the invisible population of powers or divinities can penetrate even into the most hidden recesses of the human soul. And, while on the one hand this provides rulers with an instrument through which they can attribute to themselves the ability of overseeing even the most intimate reasons that drive the lives of individuals, on the other hand it engenders in individuals the terrifying idea that not even their innermost thoughts can escape the scrutiny of an unappealable Judge. It is a situation in which it appears impossible to evade the prescribed compliance.

But controlling intentions does not eliminate the unintended consequences; and everyone's life remains always exposed to unplanned and unpredictable events. Therefore, to transform what happens unexpectedly into an intentional product, it becomes necessary to imagine a new intervention of the invisible powers or a conflict between them, to which one can attribute what has unexpectedly occurred. The actions of the divinities are changeable and, in addition, the divinities can oppose each other. Thus, when the event has an unpredictably negative character, it is attributed to the prevalence of hostile forces and, when it has an unexpectedly positive character, it is attributed to the prevalence of benevolent forces. This is why, referring to Greek polytheism, David Hume wrote: "the conduct of events, or what we call the plan of a particular providence, is so full of variety and uncertainty that, if we suppose it immediately ordered by any intelligent beings, we must acknowledge a contrariety in their designs and intentions in the same power, from impotence or levity".[18] Discussing the same issue, Max Weber in turn recalled that the Greeks sacrificed "to Aphrodite and Hera alike, to Dionysus and Apollo"; they imagined that such deities were "frequently in conflict with one another";[19] and attributed the outcome of actions to the prevailing will of the gods who presided over the "various value spheres of the world" or, ultimately, to the mysterious action of the Moiras.[20]

The terms in which Hume and Weber put the issue leads to Greek tragedy.[21] And this shows us that, even from the most consistent behaviour, something can be born which "is not beautiful and not holy and not good".[22] Good does not only stem from good; and evil does not always produce evil. Quite often the opposite is true.[23] Alongside or instead of what we intend to pursue, actions permanently produce unintended consequences. Life is subject to the most varied vicissitudes. It is significant that, to explain the concept of "peripeteia", Aristotle referred to Sophocles' *Oedipus Rex*: "Peripeteia is a change by which a train of action produces the opposite of the effect intended [...]. Thus, [...] the messenger comes to cheer Oedipus and free him from his alarms about his mother but, by revealing who Oedipus is, he produces the opposite effect."[24]

Greek tragedy is therefore centred on the unintended outcomes of human actions; and, through this, it exposes in a paradigmatic way the vicissitudes to which every human being is subject. Our condition is utterly insignificant. Although we act deliberately, the consequences generated by our actions do not always correspond to our expectations; and often they thwart them completely. In Greek tragedy, this occurs because our will clashes with the will of divine powers, devised in the image and likeness of humanity, who live invisibly above us and who tower over us. The unintended outcomes of human actions are the intentional outcomes of the actions of a divine population. Herein lies the reason why Greek tragedy was from its inception "a sacred office, part of the state cult, and it remained so as long as it had a life of its own".[25]

As Max Pohlenz wrote, "contained in the religious faith [of the Athenians ...] was the belief that in the spiritual and moral world there existed an order [...] founded by the great father Zeus".[26] This does not, however, prevent us from seeing that, whatever the order which is ultimately established, it is not the predictable result of the application of a known norm, capable of guaranteeing equal treatment to all and in all cases. There are outcomes which come from provisional decisions, from second thoughts and even from the whims of the gods themselves.[27] "Ethical paradoxes" occur again and again.[28] And tragedy involves "innocent guilt", a situation in which human beings act, but are not "masters" of their "fate":[29] they "become guilty, by performing a guiltless action".[30] Therefore, it can be said that "the characters [...] are not men, but superhuman powers".[31] Faith must be so strong that it can bridge the indecipherability of the principle on the basis of which divinity acts;[32] and so strong that it can sustain the break that is caused whenever the human aspiration to justice is countered by the injustice perpetrated by divine will.

The tragedies of Euripides, however, provided a forewarning of something that was happening. As Friedrich Nietzsche wrote, the

> spectator now virtually saw and heard his double on the Euripidean stage, and rejoiced that he could talk so well. But this joy was not all: one even learned of Euripides how to speak: he prides himself upon this in his answer with Aeschylus: how the people have learned from him how to observe, debate, and draw conclusions according to the rules of art and with the cleverest sophistications [...]. Civic mediocrity, on which Euripides built all his political hopes, was now suffered to speak, while heretofore the demigod in tragedy and the drunken satyr, or demiman, in comedy, had determined the character of the language.[33]

Nietzsche also claimed that tragedy "died by suicide".[34] But that was not what actually happened. Faith in the gods of Olympus could not have withstood opening up to the world. José Ortega y Gasset wrote:

> The experience to which a *people* like the Athenians, who were [...] intensely integrated in their traditional beliefs, were subjected was a deeply shattering one. The *intellectual* delay, which coincided with its political triumph over Greece and the sudden and extraordinary growth of its wealth, meant that it received, all arriving at the same time in the squares and porticoes of Athens, what had brewed in the rest of Hellas in the course of a century and a half.

The "new Ionian, Pythagorean, Eleatic science" arrived; "models of geometric bodies and armillary spheres" were lifted from crates; "eclipses were explained as facts which were extremely simple and devoid of any mystery [...]. There was heard the terrible blasphemy that the stars were not deities, but spheres of incandescent metal."[35] Protagoras stated that "man is the measure of all things" and that, as for the gods, no one is in the position to ascertain "whether they are, or whether they are not", since this is hindered by "the obscurity of the matter and the brevity of human life".[36]

This "way of thinking represented the complete reversal of the mythical *logos* from which the gods were born".[37] The compact and rapt universe of the old tragedy collapsed. A "rift" opened up, caused by the split between "culture and religion".[38] This means that, contrary to Nietzsche's claims, tragedy did not commit suicide; the conditions that made it possible or, more precisely, that made that type of tragedy possible gave way.

There was "in Athens, and even more in Piraeus", a "strange mixture of language and dialect, of clothes and ways of life".[39] Travel and trade had shattered the old myths and replaced them with critical discussion. The market was the main economic institution. "Everything that was scarce was expensive, and vice versa; in case of urgent need one had to sell cheaply. The ordinary law of supply and demand ruled."[40] The Athenians "never aimed at economic self-sufficiency"; their lives, "neither in peace, nor in war", were guided by the idea "of protecting Attic production against imports from abroad".[41] This entailed political consequences. The inhabitants of Piraeus were the most democratic of the citizens proper.[42] And there occurred a transition from "subjection of the individual to the State" to "freedom from the State, to the autonomy of the person".[43] That is why there are so many who argue that it was in Athens that there first appeared the "liberty of the moderns", namely individual freedom of choice.[44]

1.3 THE "GOVERNMENT OF MEN" (AND OF THE GODS) AND THE "GOVERNMENT OF THE LAW"

If we bear all this in mind, then we understand the reason why the age of Pericles was the time which saw "the grandest movement in the *profane* annals of mankind";[45] and the question resides precisely in the "profane" history of man. Mythological fantasies made it possible to transform unintended consequences, whether good or bad, into the intentional actions of an invisible population of deities. Thus, the final result was understood as being an intentionally determined order (*taxis*). Behind events, there always was a conscious will: if something escaped the Great Legislator, the "intercessor" between God and man, divine intervention would have occurred. And yet, if one renounces the old religious beliefs, how is it possible to provide an explanation of what socially is not the product of some human will?

Ortega y Gasset wrote that "all the Greeks [...] were blind to the reality which we today call s*ociety*".[46] But the Athenians well understood the function of the law.[47] As Jaeger pointed out, "in the heroic age of the Athenian democracy [...] *isonomy* was the supreme ideal, a social order based on equality before the law. It was the *pólis* which represented this principle and protected the freedom of the individual against powerful pressure groups".[48] The basis of this was the law, "not a mere decree but the *nomos*".[49] And, even "in the period of gradual dissolution of the old Greek faith in law", the "strict relationship of the *nomos* to the nature of the *cosmos* was not universally questioned".[50]

In this situation, the social order, the compatibility of actions, that is, is not something that is deliberately decided and imposed by the rulers and/or the deities.[51] It is the outcome of a process of "composition" made possible by the law, the task of which is to mark out the spheres of autonomy of individuals and to prevent them from harming each other.

Since it is populated by individuals with differing philosophical and religious conceptions, the open world is the place of choice; and this eliminates the possibility that the contents of actions be determined in a prescriptive manner.[52] The social order is established in an unintended way: because it is the result of the concurrence of actions which are individually decided and directed to other purposes (we obviously cannot know in advance its concrete configuration).[53] In other words: the autonomy of the individual subjects generates intentional outcomes and unintended outcomes (in relation to the individual actors, unintended outcomes may have a positive or negative character). But the overall order has an unintended character (*cosmos*). It is not attributable to the will of anyone in particular. It is the fruit of the "composition" of an infinite number of social relations, of which the abstract order of the law is the indispensable condition.[54] Openness to the world, choice, law and unintended order go hand in hand.

Various positions have emerged in relation to this. Protagoras was an advocate of an open society and a friend of Pericles; he saw in what we now call voluntary social cooperation the only means by which human beings can remedy their inadequacy. Socrates was a critic of Athenian democratic institutions. "But there is no need for a man who criticizes democracy and democratic institutions to be their enemy, although both the democrats he criticizes, and the totalitarians who hope to profit from any disunion in the democratic camp, are likely to brand him as such."[55] In fact, as Popper wrote, Socrates made a "great contribution" to faith in an open society;[56] and, precisely because of that faith, he lost his life.[57] "Socratic non-knowledge" is the basis of the "equalitarian theory of human reason".[58] It therefore excludes that there can be any privileged source of knowledge, any "privileged point of view on the world". It thus removes all possible legitimation for the claim to impose a compulsory hierarchy of ends; prevents the concept of justice from being formulated in positive terms; and only makes it possible to identify what is not "just".

But at that time there was something else as well. Eduard Meyer reminded us: "political theories sprout like mushrooms. Even though they bring exceptional new proposals, everyone agrees that they seek their ideal in the past, in the antique aristocratic constitution, in the governments of Crete and Sparta, even in monarchy; and they decidedly and disdainfully move away from Athenian democracy".[59] Meyer added: "This reactionary theory has [...] crudely formulated and adopted the concept [...] that the citizen with full rights must be materially independent, that manual labour is to be discredited, and that money transactions and mortgages with interest are uncivil and should be forbidden".[60] In short, the common denominator of those writings was the desire to suppress the "open society", to restore in some way the lost order.

1.4 PLATO AND THE NEW INTENTIONAL ORDER

Among the reactionary theories to which Meyer referred, we can largely include Plato's. The founder of the Academy placed himself in a position opposite to Protagoras. Whereas Protagoras maintained that "man is the measure of all things", Plato stated the exact opposite; namely, that "god is the measure of all things".[61] However, he proposed replacing the old religious beliefs with other ones. This was clarified in exemplary manner by George Grote:

> Plato does not pretend to substitute truth in place of fiction; but to furnish a better class of fictions in place of a worse. The religion of the Commonwealth, in his view, is to furnish fictions and sanctions to assist the moral and political views of the lawgiver, whose duty it is to employ religion for this purpose.[62]

Not unlike Critias, Plato saw in religious beliefs a "lordly lie" by means of which to keep the governed under control.[63]

The "intercessor" with God now became the philosopher. For Plato stated: "the human race will never cease from ills, until the race of those who philosophize correctly and truly shall come to political power, or the persons of power in state, by a certain divine allotment, philosophize really".[64] "We must make the most perfect philosophers guardians."[65] Consequently, the philosopher is the bearer of the word of God, of a knowledge to which all must submit.

But Plato went further. Let us first focus on his ideal society. Plato fuelled the illusion of being able to place "man in a universe that in its perfect order and harmony was an eternal model for the life" of human beings.[66] This means that we must not make the frequently made mistake, of seeing in him a thinker who is simply "authoritarian, favouring the autocracy of the wise".[67] Plato conferred a "new spirit" on the "materials" provided by Spartan reality.[68] He indicated as his goal a society in which the will and desire of each are not incompatible with the will and desire of others. And the point is that, if this objective were attainable, this would mean a liberation from all kinds of scarcity (not only from that relating to material goods) and an end to all forms of conflict: a situation in which there would no longer be unintended consequences; and there would no longer be tragedy, not only the Greek form, but tragedy in general. As Max Scheler acutely wrote, "in a world that was part of an 'ethical, cosmic order', in a world in which human powers were directed according to the needs of unification and harmony, tragedy would be impossible".[69] A brief consideration of Jacob Burckhardt's may be of assistance. It reads: "It is already quite astonishing that Plato has considered truly possible for his ideal of state or society to be realised; but in our eyes he fabricates [...] a suitable religion" to make the realization credible.[70]

Truly, it is hard to credit that Plato could have believed in the erection of "perfect harmony". But the religion he propounded, just as Burckhardt maintained, provides faith in the possibility of reaching the goal: because it does not give the believer a simple privileged knowledge; it gives a salvific knowledge, knowledge, that is, that eradicates evil and that realizes the definitive Kingdom of Good. Thus, the philosopher is not only the "intermediary" between God and man. He is the "redeemer" of humanity.[71]

All types of private worship must be abolished: "Shrines of the gods no one must possess in a private house; and if anyone is proven to possess and worship at any shrine other than the public shrines [...], he that notices the fact shall inform the Law-wardens [...who] shall impose upon them the due penalties for their impiety."[72]

> The following law should be enacted for all cases without exception. No one shall possess a shrine in his own house: when anyone is moved in spirit to do sacrifice, he shall go to the public places to sacrifice, and he shall hand over his oblation to the priests and priestesses to whom belong the consecrations; and he himself, together with any associates he may choose, shall join in the prayers.[73]

But "there are souls inhabiting our earth", who are "bestial souls".[74] The philosopher "will take the city and the characters of men, as they could a tablet, and wipe it clean".[75] In other words: a "purgation" is necessary.[76]

> The best method of all, like the most potent medicine, is painful; it is that which effects correction by combination of justice with vengeance, in the last instance, to the point of death or exile, usually with the result of clearing society of its most dangerous members, great and incurable offenders.[77]

The rulers are similar to the gods only if they are like "commanders of armies or they may even resemble physicians defending the body from onslaughts of disease".[78]

Unintended consequences do not vanish. They are no longer transformed into intentional outcomes resulting from the intervention of a plurality of deities. They are now the intentional result which is the dualistic clash between earthly powers. Those who hold public power represent the forces of good; and those who do not abide by the prescriptions of the rulers or who, more simply, have to act as scapegoats to be blamed for the inevitable failure to achieve "perfect harmony", embody the forces of evil. This means that "such a city is not one, but two, the one of poor men, the other of rich men, who are living on the same spot and ever conspiring against one another":[79] because, "when riches and virtue are placed together in the scales of the balance, the one always rises as the other falls".[80]

We are faced here with an incorrect causal imputation, directed towards producing extremely precise effects.[81] To claim that the responsibility for all evil is to be attributed to the conscious action of the wicked and that it is possible, through the elimination of those persons, to free man from all its "cursed problems", is nothing less than a declaration of war.[82] It is not therefore the dualistic structure of society that determines the conflict; it is rather the conflict, the declared war on evil, that determines the dualistic structure.

The point is that all the projects that set out to achieve the Kingdom of Good promise a "final solution". And yet, since the goal is unattainable, they need to impose a continuous mobilization, implement a permanent extermination of their supposed enemies and saboteurs. Having rightly identified the seed of totalitarianism in the desire to achieve the complete suppression of evil, Popper did not hesitate to qualify the thought of the founder of the Academy as totalitarian and to recognize it as the true forefather of all the representatives of the totalitarian family.[83] The fact that the Platonic design made use of the "lordly lie" of religion and that the totalitarian regimes of the twentieth century resorted to a philosophy of history, does not detract from what is asserted here: knowledge is always salvific and the goal is in all cases the re-shaping of man and the world.

Popper also specified that those who "exalt Plato's reputation as a teacher of morals and announce to the world that his ethics is the nearest approach to Christianity before Christ, are preparing the way for totalitarianism and especially for a totalitarian [...] interpretation of Christianity".[84] An example is given by Augustine of Hippo, who did not conceal his links with the works of Plato. Indeed, he wrote:

> if those men [Plato and his followers] had been able to live their lives again with us, they would have seen immediately to whose authority people could more easily turn for such advice, and with a few changes here and there in their word and assertions, they would become Christian, as indeed several Platonists have done in recent times and our days.[85]

Augustine also presented society in a dualistic form. He wrote: "because some live according to flesh and others according to the spirit, there have arisen two cities [...]; we could equally well have said: because some live according to man, others according to God".[86]

Obviously, as in any form of monotheism, conflict can only be dualistic. The problem arises, however, when there is the temptation to build the divine city on this earth, through the elimination of the wicked, who are often simply those who have a different opinion from ours. In this case, we are faced with the claim to impose a salvific creed such as compulsory cogency. Which is exactly what all forms of totalitarianism are based on.

1.5 UNINTENDED CONSEQUENCES AS THE OBJECT OF THE SOCIAL SCIENCES

Nothing can shelter human life from the unintended consequences produced by our own actions. Transforming them into the intentional results of the intervention of a population of invisible deities or the clash between the equally invisible forces of good and evil, means blatantly side-stepping the problem: because man remains "inexorably bound to the sole and decisive reality of divine will";[87] and "what happens [...] depends on the arbitrary power [...], on the inscrutable and inescapable decrees of God".[88] Placed in such a situation, human beings cannot "reason, analyse, compare, infer, control, conclude". "The first thing they [... must] do is pray, direct a prayer to God, so that they may be enlightened".[89] All there is to be done is to "implore God to reveal his decrees".[90]

We must therefore abandon the idea that the outcomes we have not planned are due to the intentional intervention of invisible powers. It is also necessary to avoid the temptation of transcribing the "plan" of "theological origin" in a secularized form, where everything occurs on account of an equally mysterious intentionality;[91] this drives us to entrust ourselves to the will of an individual human being, who is in some way the holder of privileged knowledge, which he changeably provides to those who show a greater herd vocation. Such situations preclude, or forcefully hinder, the emergence of the social sciences. In order for them to take root and flourish, it is necessary to embrace a different outlook. It needs to be recognized that no one can ever escape error and one must come to terms with the problem of unintended consequences.[92]

Émile Durkheim pointed out appropriately that, if he remains "endowed" with the capacity he is believed to have "to devise, modify and discard laws as he pleases" and an "almost limitless power", the Great Legislator, even when removed from a union with the divinity, represents a real "superstition";[93] and added that "nothing has so retarded social science as this point of view".[94] On the other hand, addressing natural law and contractualist theories, Werner Sombart wrote that the "founders of modern sociology need to be sought among the staunchest opponents of jusnaturalism and contractualistic theory".[95]

What is the problem? Just as we cannot attribute omniscience to any man, we cannot even suppose that everyone knows everything: there is no "manifest truth", of which everyone is the bearer and which allows everyone to know what it is possible and what it is impossible to do.[96] Thus, if we embrace the idea that whatever is not directly willed by us is attributable to the action of an extraordinary man or extraordinary men, we remain within a conception that makes it possible to transform unintended events into intentional events. And, if we attribute the ability to know what it is possible and what it is impossible to do to the generality of human beings, we must necessarily accept that every social event is an intentional product of human action. Here too, we deny the very existence of unintended consequences;[97] and we set up a situation in which every social rule or institution becomes superfluous, because it contradicts the premise of omniscience.[98]

To argue that the social order is directly determined by human will (whether of a single man or of all men) does not allow us to answer the problem.[99] We must therefore turn our backs not only on the intentional order willed by the divinity (or the divinities); we must also reject the secularized transcription of the plan of theological origin. But this, while necessary, is not enough. The pars *construens* consists in recognizing: (a) that the action of each produces a sequence of outcomes that escapes the control of any actor; (b) that it is necessary to shed light on the process that makes human actions the source of unplanned events, which occur in addition to or instead of the goals set; and (c) that it is necessary to identify the conditions that make it possible to correct the actions from which unintended consequences of a negative character ensue: conditions which spare unintended consequences of a positive character and which make possible a social order which is not intentionally pursued.

In a short, but highly influential, paper, Robert K. Merton drew the attention of scholars to the matter of the unanticipated consequences of purposive social action. He recalled certain terms by which the entire issue had been indicated or with which certain of its aspects had been identified in the course of time. We repeat some of them here: Providence (immanent or transcendent); Moira; Paradoxie der Folgen; Schicksal; social forces; heterogony of ends.[100] Merton also provided a list of authors who in some way engaged with the problem or stumbled upon it. These include Adam Smith and Max Weber. But not Pierre Bayle, Bernard de Mandeville, David Hume, Charles-Louis de Montesquieu, Josiah Tucker, David Ferguson, Edmund Burke, Benjamin Constant, François Guizot, Herbert Spencer, Carl Menger and Georg Simmel; whereas authors who had a later and less significant relationship with the issue are included.[101] We shall see in the following pages how the study of unintended consequences came to coincide with the birth of the social sciences.[102]

NOTES

1. Aristotle (B), 1322b.
2. Fustel de Coulanges ([1864] 1877), p. 232.
3. Spencer ([1877–1896] 1906), vol. 2, p. 722.
4. Frazer (1925), p. 9. What Frazer argued is exactly what had previously been argued by Fustel de Coulanges ([1864] 1877, p. 208): "the ancient kings of Greece and Italy were priests". Referring to Fustel de Coulanges, Ortega y Gasset ([1960] 1946–83e, p. 126) wrote that the *rex* is the "rector", the one who "rules or directs religious rites".
5. Frazer (1925), p. 10.
6. Op. cit., p. 52.
7. Ibid.
8. Malinowski (1948), p. 57.
9. Frazer (1925), p. 52.

10. Ibid. It can also be mentioned that Malinowski (1948, p. 68) stated that magic is a "practical art consisting of acts which are only means to a definite end expected to follow later on". He then added that religion is instead "a body of self-contained acts being themselves the fulfillment of their purpose"; however, affirming that religious acts are themselves the realization of their purpose is a very weak thesis, which deprives religion of its cause. Not surprisingly, Malinowski also admitted that religious beliefs are an instrument "in the struggle with the difficulties and at the prospect of death" (op. cit., p. 69).
11. Resorting to a term coined by Tylor (1903, vol. 2, p. 108), one can say that magic and religion are thus used to attribute events not directly derivable from human action to "personified" causes in any case. We are in the realm of psychomorphism or anthropomorphism. See also Tarde (1895), p. 266.
12. Malinowski (1948), p. 67.
13. Op. cit., p. 14.
14. Op. cit., p. 69.
15. Precisely for this reason, the sacred is at the same time *mysterium tremendum* and *mysterium fascinans* (see Otto, 1926, pp. 13–54). Ortega y Gasset ([1958] 1946–83f, p. 212) wrote: "the gods always have two faces: they are irascible and they are propitious, they are hostile and they are favorable, they are frightful and they are seductive".
16. Popper (1991), p. 72.
17. Op. cit., pp. 342–343.
18. Hume ([1757] 1889), p. 8.
19. Weber ([1919] 1970a), p. 123.
20. Weber ([1919] 1970b), p. 147.
21. However, it is worth recalling what Jaeger wrote (1965, vol. 1, p. 241): "Epic and tragedy are two mountain-chains, connected by an unbroken line of foothills."
22. Weber ([1919] 1970b), pp. 147–148.
23. Weber ([1919] 1970a), p. 123. Guizot ([1828] 1885, p. 145) had previously written: "In everything, there is such a deep, so invincible mixture of good and evil that, whatever side you enter from, when you descend into the ultimate elements of society or of the soul, you find inside them these two orders of facts which coexist."
24. Aristotle (C), 1452a. See more extensively Romilly (1970), pp. 42–43.
25. Pohlenz (1954), p. 32.
26. Op. cit., p. 144.
27. The gods can be capricious, because their lives are shielded from the irreparability of time and choices.
28. The expression "ethical paradoxes" is Weber's ([1919] 1970a), p. 125.
29. Romilly (1970), p. 101.
30. Scheler (1923), p. 269.
31. Jaeger (1965), vol. 1, p. 255.
32. Op. cit., p. 144. 256. Jaeger himself (op. cit., p. 283) wrote that, like the riddle of the Sphinx, the enigma of divine will cannot be solved by any "mortal mind".
33. Nietzsche ([1872] 1909), p. 88. Another statement makes Nietzsche's thought even clearer: "Odysseus, the typical Hellene of the Old Art, sank, in the hands of the new poets, to the figure of the Graeculus, who, as the good-naturedly cunning domestic slave, stands henceforth in the center of dramatic interest" (op. cit., pp. 87–88).
34. Op. cit., p. 86.

35. Ortega y Gasset ([1960] 1946–83c), pp. 424–425. As is well known, it was Anaxagoras who maintained that "the sun is stone, and the moon is earth". In *The Laws*, Plato makes the Athenian answer Kleinias as follows: "as to our younger generation and their wisdom, I cannot let them off when they do mischief. For do but mark the effect of their words: when you and I argue for the existence of the gods, and produce the sun, moon, stars and earth, claiming for them a divine being, those who have been persuaded by the aforesaid philosophers will say that they are earth and stones only, which can have no care at all of human affairs, and that religion is a cooking up of words and a make-believe" (Plato [C], 886d).
36. Protagoras (A), 1.
37. Ortega y Gasset ([1960] 1946–83c), p. 421.
38. Jaeger (1965), vol. 1, p. 301. Not by chance Pohlenz (1954, p. 155) wrote: "the moral criticism levelled against the individual figures of the gods and the myths that arose in an era in which no ethical gauge was yet used with regard to superhuman beings became increasingly effective". For his part, Ehrenberg (1951, p. 267) stated: "Religion has lost a good deal of its power, at least for many; good humour and the jests of naive believers have turned into the irony of unbelievers." See also Ehrenberg (1996), pp. 358–363.
39. Ehrenberg (1951), p. 152. Ehrenberg's statement is based on what was asserted by Pseudo-Xenophon (A, II, 7–8), mainly considered to be Critias, the future leader of the Thirty Tyrants: "because they rule the sea, they have discovered different kinds of festival foods by mingling with different people in different places. Whatever is pleasing in Sicily, Italy, Cyprus, Egypt, Lydia, Pontus, the Peloponnese, or anywhere else, all these have been brought together in one place through rule of the sea. Again, they listen to every kind of dialect, and take something from one, something from another. The Greeks in general tend to keep to their own dialect, way of life, and dress, whereas the Athenians mix theirs from all the Greeks and barbarians." See also what Pericles declared in his famous *Funeral Oration*, delivered after the first year of the Peloponnesian war (Thucydides, A, II, 38).
40. Ehrenberg (1951), p. 225. See also Polanyi (1977), pp. 165–173.
41. Ehrenberg (1951), p. 141.
42. Aristotle (B), 1303b.
43. Pohlenz (1954), p. 154. In another work of his, Pohlenz (1947, p. 116) wrote: there appeared "the fundamental principle of modern liberalism", according to which "each citizen, inside the body of the state, must maintain their freedom to act and think autonomously and promptly express their own opinions, while the State should meddle as little as possible in the private lives of individuals". See also Glotz (1929), p. 142.
44. The forerunner of these authors can be considered Benjamin Constant (cf. Infantino, 2003, pp. 12–13; 2019, pp. 49–84).
45. Acton (1877), p. 11, emphasis added.
46. Ortega y Gasset ([1948] 1946–83d), p. 13. Ortega y Gasset (ibid.) added that "Aristotle, with his surprising sensitivity to the facts", had perceived "delicately that state and society are not the same thing". See Aristotle (B), 1252b–1253a.
47. Not unlike critical discussion, the law was also imported from Ionia. In this connection, Jaeger wrote: "Throughout" his "life and work, it is clear that Solon was deeply influenced by Ionian civilization. Accordingly, we cannot doubt that these new political ideas also originated in Ionia, the intellectual and critical centre

of Greece" (Jaeger, 1965, vol. 1, p. 99; see also p. 442, note 20). On the Greek origin of many Roman legal institutions, see Jhering ([1872] 1965, p. 440).
48. Jaeger (1947), pp. 360–361. See also Huizinga (1945), p. 95.
49. Jaeger (1947), p. 361.
50. Op. cit., p. 365.
51. It is no coincidence that Biscardi (1982, pp. 355–356) stated: "this new justice presupposes the, at least tendentially democratic, *autonomy*, of the *polis*, namely the transition from an aristocratic society to a community of equals, in which the citizens obey the laws [...] since they lay them down, if only in the sense that they freely accept the established order, of which they consider themselves to be an integral and active part. For, whereas in the aristocratic society there reigned the principle of *heteronomy*, so that the ordering party was placed outside the community, now *nomos* becomes a force that moves from within." The social one is an "inner bond", it is not the product of external intervention (see Simmel, [1900] 1978, p. 175). This shows how unfounded the thesis supported by Malinowski (1926, p. 66) is, according to which the "rules of a Melanesian community correspond to our civil law". He was not deterred by the fact that, in that population, the law did not constitute an "independent, self-contained social arrangement" (op. cit., p. 59), nor by the consideration that, in that same context, the idea of a "general" and "abstract" norm was inconceivable (op. cit., p. 42). Malinowski made everything hinge on the concept of "reciprocity". But all social norms perform the function of co-adapting actions. Therefore, "reciprocity" is not only a feature of legal rules. The point is that, as a general and abstract rule, law cannot exist in a sacral-magical world, dominated in an all-pervasive way by prescription and by what this entails in terms of arbitrariness and the impossibility of institutionalizing individual choice.
52. Jaeger (1965, vol. 1, p. 104) specified: "Every trifling dispute above *meum* and *tuum* called for a standard by which the claims of the parties could be measured. This is the same problem in the sphere of law as that which had, in the same age, been solved in the economic sphere by the introduction of fixed standards of weight and measure for the exchange of goods. What was needed was a correct norm to measure legal rights, and that norm was found in the concept of equality". See also Palmer (1950, pp. 149–168); Biscardi (1982, p. 354); Paoli (1933, pp. 177–186; 1976, pp. 31–78).
53. See more extensively Infantino (2020a), pp. 123–128 and the bibliography indicated therein.
54. Weber ([1922] 1978), vol. 2, p. 657; Hayek (1982), vol. 1, pp. 35–54.
55. Popper (1966), vol. 1, p. 189.
56. Ibid.
57. It is worth pointing out that, if Socrates was sent to his death by the restored democracy, under the government of the Thirty Tyrants he had been summoned by Critias and Charicles, who had ordered him to suspend his teaching (Xenophon [A], I, 2, 31–38).
58. Popper (1966), vol. 1, p. 189.
59. Meyer (1895), p. 33. See also Popper (1966), vol. 1, pp. 187–188.
60. Meyer (1895), p. 33.
61. Plato (C), 716c.
62. Grote (1867), vol. 3, p. 187.
63. On the use by Plato and his followers of religion as a means of social control, cf. Aristotle (A), 1074b, 1–5. The expression "lordly lie" is Popper's (1966,

vol. 1, p. 142). But Plato himself (B, 389b) stated: "if, as we are saying, a lie is useless to the gods, and useful only as a medicine to men, then the use of such medicine should be restricted to physicians; private individuals have no business with them"; and, later (op. cit., 414b), he spoke of "lordly lie" or, as it is also sometimes translated, of "royal lie". On the contiguity, in religious matters, between the ideas of Critias and those of Plato, again see Popper (1966, vol. 1, pp. 141–142); Jaeger (1965, vol. 1, p. 330); Bultrighini (1999, pp. 242– 248).
64. Plato (D), 326a–b.
65. Plato (B), 503b, see also 501e.
66. Jaeger (1961), p. 66.
67. Friedrich (1968), p. 59.
68. Ollier (1933), p. 236.
69. Scheler (1923), p. 250. It is like saying that in Paradise tragedy would not be possible (Ortega y Gasset, [1958] 1946–83f, p. 268). Scheler (op. cit., pp. 83–84) added that it is equally obvious that a "satanic world would suppress the tragic, neither more nor less than a divine world".
70. Burckhardt (1900), vol. 2, p. 122.
71. Hoffmann (1960), p. 168.
72. Plato (C), 910c. See also 907d–e and 908a.
73. Op. cit., 909d.
74. Op. cit., 906b.
75. Plato (B), 501a.
76. Plato (C), 735c.
77. Op. cit., 735e.
78. Op. cit., 905e.
79. Plato (B), 551d.
80. Op. cit., 550e.
81. Plato attributed the inevitable social war to private property, which he called to be suppressed; in the various totalitarian programmes, the abolition of property can be replaced by its strict political control (consider Nazism). This is a reversal of reality. Private property did not originate to create conflict, but to regulate it by marking out what belongs to each social actor. It must then be clarified that depicting social life as a zero-sum game, as a relationship, that is, in which cooperation is beneficial for only one of the parties, is a representation that, taken to its logical consequences, legitimizes a war of all against all. See Infantino (2020a, pp. 23–24) and the bibliography indicated therein.
82. "Cursed problems" is an expression of Lunaciarskij's (1973), p. 205.
83. For an extensive discussion of this, see Infantino (2020a, pp. 73–78). Unlike Friedrich's claim (1968, p. 59), judging Plato's thought as totalitarian is therefore not an "unfortunate misunderstanding".
84. Popper (1966), vol. 1, p. 104.
85. Augustine (A), IV, 7, p. 34. On Augustine's debts to Plato, see Infantino (2020a, pp. 57–92) and the bibliography provided therein.
86. Augustine (B), vol. 2, XIV, 4, p. 7.
87. Ortega y Gasset ([1941] 1946–83b), p. 535.
88. Ibid.
89. Ibid.
90. Op. cit., p. 536.
91. Dilthey ([1883] 1959), p. 98. Dilthey went on to point out (op. cit., p. 100) that "every attempt [...] to show the plan and meaning of human history is only

a transformation of the old [theological] system: the education of the human race indicated by Lessing, the self-development of God celebrated by Hegel, the Comtian transformation of hierarchical organization are nothing else". Dilthey also included in this group the philosophies of history expounded by Turgot and Kant.

92. Popper (1991, p. 29) rightly wrote that "our knowledge can be only finite, while our ignorance must necessarily be infinite".

93. Durkheim ([1966] 1980), p. 11. A superior being and a bearer of privileged knowledge, the Great Legislator testifies with his unique presence that what happens in society does not respond to any predefined law. There is therefore no knowledge accessible to others through an open process, in which everyone can actively participate. This makes social life the permanent place of the *extraordinary*, deciphered only by an *extraordinary* man, who cannot be asked to limit his power; on the contrary, it must be made unlimited. In such a habitat, there obviously exist none of the conditions that make critical discussion and the birth of the social sciences possible. Durkheim's criticism of the Great Legislator was preceded by Comte's. We will focus on this in Chapter 5, Section 5.3. However, not unlike Comte, Durkheim ([1928] 1962, pp. 72–73) remained tied to the idea that society should be held together by a "common sensorium". For a comprehensive discussion of the problem, see Infantino (1998), pp. 57–99.

94. Durkheim ([1966] 1980), p. 12.

95. Sombart (1923), p. 9. This did not deter Sombart from the temptation to write in another work, *Die drei Nationalökonomien*, which is full of invectives against economic theory, that Hitler took orders directly from God, the supreme *Führer* of the universe (Sombart, [1934] 1937, p. 194). See more extensively Mises (1978), pp. 102–103.

96. Popper (1991, p. 5. As there is no privileged source of knowledge (men are all equally ignorant and fallible), there is no general omniscience (human beings can be considered equal not as a result of what they know, but because of their common condition of ignorance and fallibility).

97. As Popper (1991, p. 17) rightly pointed out, if truth is "manifest", ignorance becomes a guilty "conspiracy". Furthermore, in the fourth of his *Metaphysical Meditations*, Descartes ([1641] 1901b, p. 180) argued that errors arise from the "will", which is "much ampler and more extended than the understanding". As Ortega y Gasset ([1923] 1946–83a, pp. 159–160) observed, such "audacity" leads to the conclusion that, "if it were not for the sins of the will, the first man would already have discovered all acquirable truths; there would therefore not have been any variety of opinions, laws, customs; in short, there would not have been any history". And "history would substantially be the history of human errors [...]. History and life are charged with a negative sense, like something criminal."

98. Hayek (1982), vol. 2, p. 20.

99. Consequently, there are steps which we cannot avoid. First of all, we must renounce the "privileged point of view of the world". This idea necessarily leads to the search for an individual or a social group that holds this knowledge (cf. Popper, 1991, p. 24); suffice it to recall Plato's philosopher-king, Saint-Simon's "industrialists", Hegel's "general class", Comte's "scientific class", Marx's "proletariat", Durkheim's "sui generis" class and Hitler's "race". And we must also abandon the illusion of a "manifest truth" possessed or acquired by everyone.

100. Merton (1936), p. 894, note 3.
101. Op. cit., footnote 1.
102. It is useful to quote here what was written on this subject by Hayek (1979, p. 69): "If social phenomena showed no order except insofar as they were consciously designed, there would indeed be no room for theoretical sciences of society and there would be, as often argued, only problems of psychology. It is insofar as some sort of order arises as a result of individual action but without being designed by any individual that a problem is raised which demands a theoretical explanation." For his part, Popper (1991, vol. 1, p. 214) wrote: "The characteristic problems of the social sciences arise only out of our desire to know the *unintended* consequences [...] which may arise if we do certain things."

2. Pierre Bayle and Bernard de Mandeville

> [...] the Republic of Letters is not a country where one can be content with good intentions. (Pierre Bayle)
>
> [...] the greatest part [of our ...] attribute is acquired, and comes upon multitudes, from their conversing with one another [...]. Men become sociable, by living together in society. (Bernard de Mandeville)

2.1 TRUE INDIVIDUALISM AND FALSE INDIVIDUALISM

The doctrine of "manifest truth" is not found only in Descartes. He "based his optimistic epistemology on the important theory of the *veracitas dei*. What we clearly and distinctly see to be true must indeed be true; for otherwise God would be deceiving us. Thus, the truthfulness of God must make truth manifest."[1] The "systematic doubt" frees us from all our "prejudices"; and puts us in a position to reach the "self-evident truth".[2]

Although apparently it may seem the opposite, Bacon's is not a different theory. "It might be described as the doctrine of the *veracitas naturae* [...]. Nature is an open book. He who reads it with a pure mind cannot misread it. Only if his mind is poisoned by prejudice, can he fall into error."[3] This means that there is a way by means of which it is possible to reach a *"certain knowledge"*.[4]

According to Popper, Bacon and Descartes did not succeed "in freeing their epistemologies from authority; not so much because they appealed to religious authority – to Nature or God – but for an even deeper reason".[5]

> In spite of their individualistic tendencies, they did not dare to appeal to our critical judgment – to your judgment, or to mine; perhaps because they felt that this might lead to subjectivism and to arbitrariness. Yet, whatever the reason may have been, they certainly were only able to replace authority – that of Aristotle or the Bible – with another. Each of them appealed to a new authority; the one to *the authority of the senses*, and the other to *the authority of the intellect*.[6]

Which made the idea of unintended order unthinkable for them. Bacon always harboured the conviction that science could be the instrument for somehow building the kingdom of God on earth;[7] and in any case the figure of the

Great Legislator dominated his mind: this is confirmed by what he said about Salomon in the *New Atlantis*.[8] For his part, Descartes did not hesitate to praise Sparta. In fact, he wrote: "to speak of human things, I believe that, if Sparta was formerly flourishing, it was not because of the excellence of each of its laws [...], but because that, having been invented by one man only, they had the same object in view".[9]

Popper observed that, despite the fallacy, the "optimistic epistemology of Bacon and of Descartes" was the "major inspiration of an intellectual and moral revolution without parallel in history";[10] he added that their theory of knowledge "became the basis of the nonconformist consciousness, of individualism, and of a new sense of man's dignity";[11] but he recognized that, alongside that epistemology, another one was affirmed, which rejected the Cartesian doubt and recovered the Socratic doubt.[12]

The path taken by Socrates in *Apology* is quite unlike that of Descartes. In this dialogue with politicians, poets and craftsmen, they are reproached for their "pretence of knowledge".[13] Referring in particular to poets, Socrates stated:

> I deduced that it was not wisdom that enabled them to write their poetry, but a kind of instinct or inspiration, such as you find in seers and prophets, who deliver all their messages without knowing in the least what they mean. It seemed clear to me that the very facts that they were poets made them think that they had a perfect understanding of all other subjects, of which they were totally ignorant.[14]

"So, I left that line of inquiry too with the same sense of advantage that I had felt in the case of the politicians."[15]

Socrates' words mean that there are no privileged sources of knowledge; there are no social individuals or groups who are inevitably bearers of truth. Therefore, we must recognize our unrelenting condition of ignorance and fallibility. This constitutes the basis for a philosophical tradition that has seen, and sees, in individual freedom of choice the means by which each can contribute to an extensive process of exploration of the unknown and the correction of errors. The latter are not something we should blame ourselves for. Our condition makes them inevitable. Identifying them is an enrichment: it shows us what we should not do. But that does not rule out other mistakes. In this way, the process always remains unfinished.

Alongside the individualism based on the doctrine of "manifest truth", there is therefore also an individualism based on the condition of ignorance and fallibility. The achievements which Popper referred to are not the result of the former, considered by Friedrich A. von Hayek to be a "false" individualism, precisely because, with its alleged possession of the truth, it denies the social process and unintended outcomes (or transforms them, especially when they are of a negative character, into the intentional product of the conspiracy of others).[16] They are the product of the latter, defined by Hayek himself as "true" individualism, which places individuals on an equal footing for what they do not know and which asks them to freely mobilize their limited and fallible knowledge and their scarce resources.[17] This is an individualism that, in addition to rejecting the assumption of omniscience, denies the idea that men, even before having acquired social status, were human. It therefore does not need to operate with a *beginning* of society. As Popper rightly pointed out here, a

> pre-social human nature, which explains the foundation of society [...], is not only an historical myth, but also, as it were, a methodological myth. It can hardly be seriously discussed, for we have every reason to believe that man or rather his ancestor was social prior to being human (considering, for example, that language, presupposes society).[18]

2.2 BAYLE: LIMITS OF KNOWLEDGE, RELIGION AND MOTIVES FOR ACTION

As is well known, the recovery of Socratic doubt preceded the affirmation of Cartesian rationalism.[19] However, the recognition of the limits to which our knowledge is subject, even if it defends us from the presumption of being able to intentionally build the social order, does not yet free us from the idea that the same order can be a product of divine will; on the contrary, it can lead us back to it. Indeed, one can see precisely in the acceptance of our condition of ignorance and fallibility a first step towards religious mystery, towards, that is, what lies beyond proofs and refutations.[20] It is therefore necessary to accept all our cognitive limits; which removes us from the presumption that the social order can be the product of human will. And we need to seek an explanation that, by avoiding referring everything to the intervention of divine power, sheds light on the process through which, with no prior planning, individual projects come to "composition". Basically, it is a question of asserting, not unlike what Galileo did in other areas, a correct delimitation of the boundaries between the territory of the profane and that of the sacred.

Pierre Bayle is the writer who can help us out.[21] In his work, he tried to remove religion from any intermingling with superstition; and he then released it from the overlapping political-social functions which manipulate and turn the believer's faith to their own advantage. Bayle himself tells the story. After the appearance of a comet, in December 1680, he found himself having to answer the questions of "many people, intrigued and alarmed", all "invariably" convinced that God produces "these great phenomena to give time to sinners to prevent with penance the evils that hang over their heads";[22] or believing that comets "are like the heralds who come from God to declare war on mankind".[23]

Bayle's initial aim was therefore to "uproot from the soul of the people the fear of comets", to remove from their appearance the "quality of warning signs of the wrath of God".[24]

"So unfounded ideas", that see a divine hand behind every human and natural phenomenon, are suggested "by poets and historians", by "tradition" and by the "philosophers" themselves, who are also led to believe that "the corruption of the world arms the hand of God".[25] But in the field of knowledge we can only follow the Socratic example: we must deny "authority" to anyone;[26] error is not a voluntary act; there are no "precautions" which can allow us to avoid it.[27] There are "absolutely involuntary errors";[28] and these can also be present in the opinions held by the majority. This is why "there is no man who does not have the right to demand that his ideas be heard, even if [… he is] the only one to have them";[29] it is up to those who listen to him "to know how to defend them with thorough examination and not with prescriptions or the prejudice of their number".[30]

Bayle tried in this way to hit two targets: the first is the continuous intermingling of religious belief and belief due to pure and simple superstition; the second is represented by the presumption of being able to attain the "manifest truth". As for the latter, he considered it impossible to free men from their passions, their misunderstandings and their mistakes. He wrote:

> the world is preserved in the condition in which we see it only because men are full of a thousand false prejudices; and, if philosophy were able to make all men act according to the clear and distinct ideas of reason, we can be very sure that mankind would soon perish. Errors, passions, prejudices and a hundred other similar defects are like a necessary evil for the world. If they were cured, men would not be of any use for this earth.[31]

This means that "truth is the despair of history no less than of philosophy".[32] No one can delude themselves that they possess it. Those who seek knowledge must rely on a long and difficult process, which never makes it possible to acquire conclusive results and which advances through a continuous correction of errors.[33]

Therefore, it is not surprising that Bayle came to deny to religion one of the social functions that is commonly recognized in it; namely, acting as a bridle on human passions. Bayle wrote: "it is groundless to argue that the vague and confused knowledge of a providence is of much use in diminishing man's corruption. It is not on this side that its usefulness must be sought; indeed, it is a much more physical than moral utility […]. It is well known what impression the thought that one fights for the salvation of temples, altars and domestic gods produces on souls, *pro aris et focis* […]. This is precisely wherein lies the usefulness of false religions in relation to the preservation of states and republics."[34]

But they are a "wholly inadequate barrier to curb the passions of man".[35] Not even the Christian religion succeeds in achieving this goal. To understand this, it is enough to examine the motives that determine the actions of men.[36] Even when one is "sincerely converted to God" and one's heart "is sanctified by the grace of the Holy Spirit", "one does not govern oneself according to the lights of conscience".[37] Consequently, one cannot deceive oneself into thinking that religion is the "rule that guides human conduct".[38] One must admit that human laws succeed in "repressing evil" more effectively than religion does.[39] And it must be recognized that "atheism does not necessarily lead to the corruption of morals".[40]

Giving pre-eminence to human laws and refuting that an atheist must inevitably be the "greatest and most incorrigible villain in the universe",[41] Bayle demolished the reasons underpinning the need to make religion an unquestionable and coercively imposed social obligation. This is the condition that allows religious faith to withdraw "into the heart of the believer",[42] to become a simple personal choice, experienced in tolerance and shared within infrasocial groups.[43] No religious confession can therefore be publicly used as a "privileged point of view on the world", which can be entrusted with the task of legitimizing rulers and, if necessary, transforming unintentionally spawned social events into events attributable to the will of an invisible population of some kind.

But this is still not enough to solve the problem. As we know, the intentional order determined by the will of an individual is the product of his prescriptions. The intentional order due to the possession, on the part of all, of the "manifest truth" does not even need to be realized; it already exists before men act, because everyone knows precisely what they can and cannot do. In both situations, the intentions behind the action and the social justification of the same, just as in the order willed by God who sees and judges the motivations of each, are posited as coinciding with each other – except in instances of "wickedness".[44]

However, the real situation is very different. By extending his vision to a broader scope than the strictly religious one, Bayle penetratingly wrote that, "when one compares the actual customs of a man" with the ideas that he commonly manifests, "one is amazed not to find any conformity between these two things".[45] And his question was: "Do you want to know the cause of this inconsistency?"[46] This is the answer:

> Man decides on a certain action rather than another not by following the general knowledge he has of what he must do, but by conforming to the particular judgment that he forms when he is on the point of acting. [... This] particular judgment may, in certain cases, be in conformity with the general ideas of what he must do, but most of the time it is not, and almost always one follows the dominant passion of

one's heart, the inclination of one's temperament, the strength of one's contracted habits, the taste and sensitivity that one has towards certain objects.[47]

It can therefore be admitted that "man is a reasonable creature";[48] but "it is no less true that he almost never acts in accordance with his own principles".[49] This also occurs with believers: "according [...] to the general idea, a man who believes in God, in heaven and hell, should do everything that he knows to be pleasing to God and nothing he knows to be unwelcome to him, while life shows us that he does quite the opposite".[50] And yet, instead of damaging social life, this "inconsistency" is a source of well-being. Bayle repeated this conviction on several occasions; and he also went so far as to assert that the strict application of Christian morality would have disastrous effects. This is borne out by the following questions: "Do you not realize that the counsels of Jesus Christ are directed to the ruin of passions and occupations, without which human society cannot survive? Do you not see that, if all men were to comply meticulously with the evangelical counsels, the whole world would turn into a Trappist abbey?"[51] If "you want a nation to be strong enough to resist its neighbours, leave the maxims of Christianity as a topic for preachers".[52]

The motives of human actions are in blatant opposition to the principles professed by individual actors. But social order is still achieved. This means that, in spite of everything, the actions are co-adapted. Bayle did not provide us with a complete explanation of how this process takes place. He only referred to the "joys of mutual exchange".[53] But it is clear that his questions and his reflections project us into an order that does not derive from anyone's intentions.

2.3 MANDEVILLE: FROM HUMAN FALLIBILITY TO UNINTENDED ORDER

Frederick B. Kaye wrote that Bayle was "by far" the greatest source of inspiration for Bernard de Mandeville.[54] Kaye also suggested that there might have been some contact between the two in Rotterdam.[55] And he did not hesitate to add that Bayle laid the "foundations" for the other's work. This does not mean that further influences were not exerted by other thinkers. Kaye mentioned in particular La Rochefoucauld.[56] But it should not be forgotten that Mandeville's mind was "steeped from early youth in the ideas of Erasmus and Montaigne", nor should it be neglected that at the time those same ideas were to some extent widespread.[57]

Not unlike Bayle, Mandeville escaped the illusion that there may exist some "authority" in the field of knowledge. That is why he did not hesitate to write:

> very few things [...] are the work of man, or of one generation; the greatest part of them is the product, the joynt labour of several ages [...]. The wisdom I speak of, is

not the offspring of a fine understanding, or intense thinking, but of sound and deliberate judgment, acquired from a long experience [...]. By this sort of wisdom, and length of time, it may be brought about, that there shall be no difficulty in governing a large city than [...] there is in weaving of stockings.[58]

And further: "Human wisdom is the child of time. It was not the contrivance of one man, nor could it have been the business of a few years."[59]

What each person knows is always very little. And we also cannot avoid fallibility. We push "our reason where we feel passion drives and self-love justifies all men, whatever their goals, providing each individual with the arguments to justify" their choices.[60]

Even those who act suitably to their knowledge, and strictly follow the dictates of their reason, are not less compelled so to do by some passion or other, that sets them to work, than others, who bid defiance and act contrary to both, and whom we call slaves to their passions.[61]

Therefore, there exists no omniscient man; and there is no omniscience from which all may benefit equally.

Knowledge is always partial and uncertain; it needs to be constantly checked. It follows that we will never free ourselves from our mistakes and that their correction is a process that always remains open. Knowing and believing are two very different things. The former is located in the territory of the profane, where everything must be subjected to the scrutiny of critical discussion; the latter is instead placed beyond proofs and refutations.[62] This is why Mandeville not only urged the "admirers of human understanding not to rely too much upon their own sufficiency"; he also specified that, as much as it may be useful to society, "philosophy is the worst guide to eternity, and ought never to be mixed with theology".[63]

Thus, we know little and, even where we think we know, we must accept our intellectual limitations, which compel us to admit our fallibility. We must also relinquish the claim to be able to erect a science of good and evil. For "the more a man knows of the world, either from reading or experience, the more he shall be convinced that [...] almost every thing [...] pleads for toleration".[64] And this makes it necessary to achieve a separation between politics and religion; it is necessary, that is, that religious belief be lived as a personal choice. It may guide the behaviour of the faithful, but it must not be established as a privileged source of knowledge, nor must it have obligatory cogency.[65]

If all this forms the basis of Mandeville's thought, the central problem is the need to explain how human actions can be mutually compatible. This may seem at first sight to be an unattainable goal, especially if one thinks that the question, already emphasized by Bayle, concerns the fracture between personal motivation and social justification of the action. To answer the problem,

Mandeville made use of the idea of unintended consequences, which is the real magnetic needle of all his work. It is better to proceed by degrees.

Mandeville wrote:

> if we examine every faculty and qualification, from and for which we judge and pronounce Man to be a sociable creature beyond other animals, we shall find that a very considerable, if not the greatest part of the attribute is acquired, and comes from multitudes, from conversing with one another. *Fabricando fabri fimus*. Men become sociable, by living together in society.[66]

And "it is hard to guess what man would be entirely untaught".[67] Which is like saying that there was no first man and no beginning of society.[68] What is properly human is a product of social interaction and the continuous work of co-adapting individual actions, behind which there is no guidance or planning by anyone.

Language itself has arisen "by slow degrees" and "length of time", without any design; this would have already pre-supposed its existence.[69] Consequently, there is no room for the hypothesis of a contractual origin of society. The stipulation of an original pact of coexistence between men who were isolated, and consequently devoid of language, is a fanciful hypothesis. It is like thinking that this could be done by "horses".[70] When the individual posed the problem of collective life, he already benefited from the social condition. In other words, social norms and institutions were not the direct product of human will.

The question here arises as to why human beings interact. Mandeville made it clear that the "cement of civil society" is made up of the needs, which feed "the almost constant solicitude [...] of every individual person" to seek the cooperation of others.[71] Society is "entirely built upon the variety of our wants" and its "whole superstructure is made up of the reciprocal services, which men do to each other".[72] Given their own inadequacy, each individual needs to continually exchange what he has for what is available to others.[73] Social cooperation is therefore the product of scarcity. In order to acquire the things to which we attach greater importance, we give up what is less important to us. Everyone cooperates voluntarily to improve their own position. It is a positive-sum game, it confers, that is, an advantage to all the actors who freely enact it.

Thus, what about the fracture between the motivation that drives us to act and the social justification with which we cover all our actions? If everyone works for themselves and for others, there is a division of labour. And in that case "neither the multitude [...], nor the individual have anything to fear".[74] Our motivations cannot affect the quality of the services we provide, because their evaluation is not up to us, but to those who are their beneficiaries. And it is on this assessment that the possibility of receiving what we need depends. Whatever our passions, our needs and our desires, what enables us to obtain the means by which we achieve our goals is only what we are capable of doing for others. As Smith wrote later, when we address our fellow men, we "never talk to them of our own necessities but of their advantages".[75] We play social roles that, precisely because they allow us to acquire the means we need, we try to perform as best as possible or in the most socially acceptable way.[76]

In light of this, one understands the reason why Mandeville suggested to subject the life of men to a double reading: on the one hand, we must see them as "necessitous" beings, who are "subject to hunger and thirst" and who have "many passions"; on the other hand, we must observe them "as parts and members of the whole society", that is, as individuals who, in order to satisfy their needs or passions and to reach their goals, must confer benefits on others.[77]

In such a situation, we intentionally exchange means, but cooperate unintentionally for the furtherance of the purposes of others; as a rule, we do not know the purposes pursued by others and, if we knew them, we might not even agree with them.[78] This is how we manage to bridge the gap between personal motivation and social justification of action. And this is how we escape the idea of intentional order and a related mandatory hierarchy of ends. In perfect harmony with Mandevillian gnoseological premises, this is a process in which we are forced, even though only "a few" are willing to admit it,[79] to change our "resolutions" and act also against our own "inclinations".[80] We never know whether our choices will turn out to be correct, or whether those that have proved to be correct until yesterday will still be correct today or tomorrow. The achievement of each person's goals is fuelled by the continuous correction of the mistakes made, which are nothing more than unintended consequences of a negative character. The plans of each person must therefore be subjected to continuous review. This is made possible by the individual's freedom of choice which, by subtracting social life from the will of a single decision-maker, mobilizes highly dispersed knowledge and spreads the risk of failure. It is the institutionalization of a process of *trial and error*. We are ignorant and fallible; we do not know where we will go; we are condemned to explore the unknown and continually correct our mistakes. And the regulatory *habitat* within which we must act is the "rule of law": because "unhappy is the people [...], whose welfare must depend on the virtues and consciences of ministers and politicians".[81]

What we have just set out is the most fruitful part of Mandeville's work. But there is another part: where the author formulated his positions in a deliberately provocative way. This is where he wrote: "all men endeavour to hide themselves, their ugly nakedness, from each other, and wrapping up the true motives of their hearts in the specious cloke of sociableness, and their concern for publick good, they are in hopes of concealing their filthy appetites and the deformity of their desires".[82] He asked himself where could one look for "those beautiful shining qualities of prime ministers, and the great favourites of princes that are so finely painted in dedications, addresses, epitaphs, funeral sermons and inscriptions"?[83] His answer was, *"There,* and no where else".[84] And he added: "the virtues of great men" are like "large China jars", which

> make a fine shew, and are ornamental even to a chimney; one would by the bulk they appear in, and the value that is set upon them, think they might be very useful, but look into a thousand of them, and you will find nothing in them but dust and cobwebs.[85]

This is the reason why the "sagacious moralists draw men like angels, in hopes that the pride at least of some will put them upon copying after the beautiful originals which they are represented to be".[86]

Reflecting on these statements, Smith spoke of "rustic" eloquence, "very apt to impose upon the unskilful";[87] and many have associated, and associate, Mandeville's name with what is deliberately exasperated in his work.[88] This has constituted, and still constitutes, an "obstacle" to the understanding of the results achieved by the author of the *Fable.*[89] We must not forget the link with Bayle. Bayle had argued that "the Republic of letters is not a country in which one can be satisfied with good intentions";[90] and he had also glimpsed the "joys of a mutual exchange". Mandeville fully accepted these indications and brought them to a high level of development. As Hayek aptly wrote, by providing transparency on the process of co-adapting individual plans and the origin of social norms and institutions, Mandeville made us understand that everything that is human is the "result of a process of evolution and not of design".[91] Herein lies the importance of his work.

2.4 MERCANTILISTS OR LIBERALS?

Although to differing extents, Bayle and Mandeville followed the path of unintended order. They did this despite their limited knowledge of economics. With a clear mercantilist outlook, Bayle wrote: "Send everywhere to discover gold, have your fleets cross the two tropics; let neither cold, nor heat, nor anything else stop the passion to get rich: you will accumulate more wealth in your country than many others. Finances will be sufficient to maintain a great fleet and a powerful army."[92] For his part, Mandeville exalted luxury and, in some passages, did so with mercantilist tones.[93]

However, one should not forget that Bayle and Mandeville were writing before Hume and Smith. And above all we need to bear in mind that the lasting value of their work is not linked to their concessions to mercantilism, but to the contribution they made to the formulation of a theory of unintended order. To clarify the matter further, it is worthwhile reviewing some of the most significant opinions expressed on Mandeville, the examination of which will allow the conclusions to be extended to Bayle as well.

Albert Schatz considered *The Fable of the Bees* to be a "capital work, in which one finds the essential elements of the economic and social philosophy of individualism".[94] And Kaye argued that a "very important aspect of Mandeville's economic speculation" is the "defence of free trade".[95] But Eli F. Heckscher was of the opposite opinion. He saw in Mandeville a representative of mercantilism; and he interpreted the well-known statement that, "private vices, by the dextrous management of a skilful politician, may be turned into publick benefits" as an assertion of the need for political control of productive activity.[96]

Jacob Viner expressed a double judgement. Initially, he wrote that "important, in preparing the way for Adam Smith, was Mandeville's [...] elaborate reasoning in support of individualism [...], resting on his famous argument that 'private vices', such as 'avarice' and luxury were 'public benefits'", conclusions "deliberately stated [...] in such manner as to make them offensive to moralists, but Smith accepted them in substance while finding a more palatable form for their expression".[97] And yet, in his introduction to a reprint of *A Letter to Dion*, originally published in 1732, Viner argued that Mandeville was "a convinced adherent of the prevailing mercantilism of his time",[98] and he added, not unlike Heckscher, that the formula "private vices, publick benefits" is "elliptical" and that the claim that, through "the dextrous management of a skilful politician", private vices can become public benefits, frees it from any "implication of laissez-faire".[99]

The discussion on the theoretical placement of Mandeville's work encompasses a great number of contributions, of which it is possible to refer to only a few.[100] What we need to understand is that references to some inadequacies, or to his misunderstanding of particular aspects of the market economy, should not prevent us from holding firm to the most important point; namely, that Mandeville put before us an entirely novel explanation of the social order. This is unequivocally borne out by his criticism of Hobbes and Shaftesbury. Despite all their differences, these authors have in common the idea of an intentionally constructed social order. And Mandeville wrote:

> It is very unworthy of a philosopher to say, as *Hobbes* did, that man is born unfit for society, and alledge no better reason for it than the incapacity that infants come into world with; but some of his adversaries have as far overshot the mark, when they asserted, that every thing which men can attain, ought to be esteemed as a cause of his fitness for society [...]. I believe neither.[101]

Insisting on the latter thinker, Mandeville went on to remark: "This noble writer (for it is the Lord *Shaftesbury* I mean in his *Characteristicks*) fancies, that as man is made for society, so he ought to be born with a kind affection to the whole, of which he is part, and a propensity to seek the welfare of it".[102] But society is not the fruit of "benevolence". Anyone who believes this falls into "utmost absurdity", relinquishes "his own understanding", and is a victim of "ignorance" and "folly".[103] "[I]f we examine into the nature of all bodies politick, we shall find, that no dependence is ever had, or stress laid on any such affection, either for the raising or maintaining of them."[104]

Some further clarifications are required. Schatz, Kaye and early Viner associated Mandeville with *laissez-faire*; Kaye in particular argued that Mandeville was one of its "forerunners".[105] And yet, if we take into account the commentary produced after the publication of the writings of these authors, this is an unacceptable association. It is tantamount to associating two "research traditions" which have a completely different outlook. Mandeville rooted his own analysis in the limits of our knowledge; he showed us the cause of the divergence between the interests of individuals; he explained that voluntary social cooperation is a game that benefits all participants; he shed light on the mechanism through which, by generating points of mediation, i.e. rules and institutions, individual plans co-adapt; he showed how, despite that which remains constant in the life of human beings and society, the ways in which we cooperate to carry out our projects are subjected to incessant change; he made clear the ateleological character of the social process; and he introduced us to cultural evolutionism.

In this context, public power can no longer have the status of an independent variable. It is true: the continuing presence of divergent interests proves that human action has an irrepressible political dimension.[106] Consequently, there is a need for an entity that prevents anyone from "exercising arbitrary coercion to the detriment of others";[107] and it is public authority which must perform this function. But this is only a necessary complement to voluntary social cooperation. It no longer dictates the contents of our lives. It must itself respect the sovereignty of the law, which is accompanied by a complex institutional structure.[108]

Laissez-faire is part of the repertoire of the French rationalist tradition. Its gnoseological postulates call upon the doctrine of "manifest truth"; this does not allow any escape from the idea of intentional order.[109] It is significant that, in a letter to André Morellet, who had sent him the project for a *Dictionnaire du Commerce*, Hume wrote:

> I see that, in your prospectus, you take care not to disoblige your economists [François Quesnay and the physiocrats], by any declaration of your sentiments; in which I commend your prudence. But I hope that in your work you will thunder

them, and pound them, and reduce them to dust and ashes! They are, indeed, the set of men the most chimerical and most arrogant that now exist [...]. I ask your pardon for saying so, as I know you belong to that venerable body.[110]

If we go into greater detail, we must note, with Joseph A. Schumpeter, that Quesnay urged upon government what really was an active policy, and not at all one of doing nothing. Moreover, in spite of his wholesale condemnation of government regulation or control, it is relevant to observe that what he actually faced were regulations that were inherited from the past and no longer fitted current conditions: the norm of laissez-faire acquires in such a case a relative significance that differs greatly from what its absolutism suggests. Finally, we must not forget that French agriculture in 1760 was not interested in protection: there was no "danger" of large wheat imports as usual phenomenon; and free trade in agricultural products would have, if anything, increased their price.[111]

Laissez-faire was actually a mere "rule of thumb".[112] And, what is worse, it was the bearer of a very unattractive design. With his usual perspicacity, Alexis de Tocqueville reminded us:

> The state, said the economists, must not only govern, it must shape the nation. It must form the mind of citizens conformably to a preconceived model. It is its duty to fill their minds with such opinions and their hearts with such feelings as it may judge necessary. In fact, there are no limits either to its rights or its powers. It must transform as well as reform its subjects; perhaps even create new subjects, if it thinks fit. "The state," says Bodeau, "moulds men into whatever shape it pleases". That sentence expresses the gist of the entire system.[113]

Thus, what is established is an intentional order.

We can therefore say that Mandeville's work has no connection with *laissez-faire*. Quite different from the "rule of thumb" are the reasons that led the author of the *Fable* to support free trade. Above all, his gnoseological postulates were very different from those of the physiocrats. His idea of unintended order is a new horizon, which marks the boundary between two opposing ways of seeing individual and collective life and which marks the birth of the social sciences.[114]

NOTES

1. Popper (1991), vol. 1, p. 7.
2. Op. cit., p. 15.
3. Op. cit., p. 7.
4. Op. cit., p. 14.
5. Op. cit., p. 15.
6. Op. cit., pp. 15–16.

7. Bacon ([1620] 1975, p. 117) did not hesitate to state that "discoveries are as it were new creations, and imitations of God's works".
8. Bacon ([1624] 1925), pp. 27–28.
9. Descartes ([1637] 1901a), p. 15.
10. Popper (1991), p. 8.
11. Ibid.
12. Op. cit., p. 16.
13. "Pretence of knowledge" is an expression used more generally by Hayek (1978), p. 23.
14. Plato (A), 22c.
15. Ibid.
16. This provides an opportunity for a clarification. Bobbio (1990, p. 117) wrote that, "more or less, all reactionary doctrines have been channelled through anti-individualism". Pellicani (1992, p. 132) commented that, "starting from strictly individualistic premises", Hobbes "justified the Leviathan-State". In order to make this issue totally clear, it must be understood that Hobbes' individualistic premises lie precisely within that individualism which Hayek termed "false" and which, in various ways, pursues the intentional realization of the social order. Consequently, the claim of Strauss (1965, p. 182) that Hobbes was the "founder of liberalism" is not acceptable. For a similar criticism, see Wolin (2006, p. 655, note 124).
17. Hayek (1949), pp. 1–33. Bartley (1984, p. 109) wrote that "modern philosophy is the story of the rebellion of one authority against another authority, and the clash between competing authorities: Far from repudiating the appeal to authority as such, modern philosophy has entertained only one alternative to the practice of basing opinions on traditional and perhaps irrational authority: namely, that basing them on" a presumably rational authority. In light of what has been said in the text, Bartley's position seems reductive, precisely because there developed a philosophical tradition, of which he himself was an exponent, which refused to replace a *foundation* with another *foundation*, that is, he rejected the doctrine of "manifest truth".
18. Popper (1966), vol. 2, p. 93.
19. Popper (1991, p. 16) counted Nicholas of Cusa, Erasmus of Rotterdam and Michel de Montaigne among those who recovered the Socratic doubt.
20. Montaigne ([1580] 1838, p. 226) had seen in the "presumption" the "natural and original disease" of the human being, considered as the "most calamitous and fragile of all creatures".
21. In relation to Bayle, Voltaire ([1752] 1822, vol. 7, p. 246) wrote: "One of the most persecuted philosophers was the immortal Bayle, honor of mankind."
22. Bayle ([1682] 1965–70a), vol. 1, p. 7.
23. Op. cit., p. 10.
24. Op. cit., pp. 5–6.
25. Op. cit., pp. 10–12. For his part, Erasmus ([1511] 1887, p. 49) had written: "[…] if we consult all historians for an account of past ages, we shall find no princes weaker, nor any people more slavish and wretched than where the administration of affairs fell on the shoulders of some learned bookish governor".
26. Bayle ([1682] 1965–70a), p. 12.
27. Op. cit., p. 68.
28. Op. cit., p. 128.
29. Op. cit., p. 22.

30. Ibid.
31. Bayle ([1685] 1965–70d), p. 274.
32. Bayle ([1683] 1965–70c), p. 53.
33. See, more extensively, Paganini (1980), p. 42.
34. Bayle ([1682] 1965–70a), p. 84.
35. Ibid.
36. Op. cit., p. 87.
37. Op. cit., p. 84 and p. 87.
38. Op. cit., p. 92.
39. Op. cit., p. 84.
40. Op. cit., p. 86.
41. Op. cit., p. 87.
42. Brega (1957), p. xiv.
43. Not unlike Montaigne, Bayle ([1697] 1820, vol. 12, p. 106) believed that, "if a man is convinced that he has no result to hope from philosophical investigations, he will feel more willing to pray to God [...], he will feel more willing [...] than those who are pleased with the successes obtained by reasoning and disputing". In recent times, Hayek (1960, p. 61) wrote: "The antirationalistic tradition is [...] close to the Christian tradition of the fallibility and sinfulness of man, while the perfectionism of the rationalistic is in irreconcilable conflict with it." On Bayle, also see Paganini (1980), p. 45.
44. In order to try to make the motivation of the action and its social justification coincide, totalitarian systems (which are the most extreme form of intentional order) resort to an all-pervasive control of every manifestation of individual life, achieved through the manipulation of language, the falsification of reality and a permanent mobilization against internal and external enemies. This is an attempt to make impossible even the most minimal forms of individual choice. Everyone's life must be completely taken up by the position they occupy in the great and terrifying political-administrative machine. See Infantino (2020a, pp. 96–105) and the bibliography presented therein.
45. Bayle ([1682] 1965–70a), p. 87.
46. Ibid. Kaye (1924, pp. xlii–xliii) traced Bayle's position back to the influence of the sceptics and, in particular, to Montaigne. In a study specifically dedicated to Bayle, Paganini (1980, p. 40) argued that "the intermediary between the complex philosophical heritage of skepticism and Bayle is certainly La Mothe Le Vayer, rather than Montaigne". However, it should be borne in mind that La Mothe Le Vayer was in turn influenced by Montaigne.
47. Bayle ([1682] 1965–70a), p. 87.
48. Ibid.
49. Ibid.
50. Ibid.
51. Bayle ([1683] 1965–70c), p. 279.
52. Bayle ([1694] 1965–70b), p. 361. This is an opportunity to quote the following passage from Swift ([1708] 2004, p. 3): "I hope no reader imagines me so weak to stand up in the defence of real Christianity, such as used in primitive times (if we may believe the authors of those ages) to have an influence upon men's belief and action. To offer at the restoring of that would indeed be a wild project; it would be to dig up foundations; to destroy at one blow all the wit, and half the learning of the kingdom; to break the entire frame and constitution of things; to

ruin trade, extinguish arts and sciences, with the professors of them; in short, to turn our courts, exchanges and shops into deserts."
53. Bayle ([1682] 1965–70a), vol. 1, p. 174. Erasmus [1511] 1887, p. 43) had already stated: "There could be no right understanding betwixt prince and people, lord and servant, tutor and pupil, friend and friend, man and wife, buyer and seller, or any persons however otherwise related, if they did not [...] put up small abuses." On another occasion, Erasmus ([1517] 1917, pp. 6–7) spoke of the need for exchange and mutual benefit for the actors involved. In today's language, we could say that he depicted the exchange as a positive-sum game.
54. Kaye (1924), p. ciii.
55. Ibid., p. cv. Kaye based his hypothesis on the fact that Mandeville attended the Erasmian School in Rotterdam, where Bayle was a teacher.
56. Ibid.
57. Hayek (1978), p. 253.
58. Mandeville ([1714–1729] 1924), vol. 2, pp. 321–322.
59. Mandeville (1732), p. 41. Mandeville's passages recall Cicero ([A], II, I): "Our own commonwealth was based upon the genius, not of one man, but of many; it was founded, not in one generation, but in a long period of several centuries and many ages of men." Cicero (ibid.) then attributed to Cato the Censor the following statement: "there never has lived a man possessed of so great genius that nothing could escape him, nor could the combined powers of all the men living at one time possibly make all necessary provisions for the future without the aid of actual experience and the test of time".
60. Mandeville ([1714–1729] 1924), vol. 1, p. 333.
61. Mandeville (1732), p. 31.
62. Mandeville (1723), pp. 64–65.
63. Op. cit., pp. 84–85. Mandeville (op. cit., pp. 181–182) also stated: "when men, having in vain raised all their faculties to render the infinite sublimity of God and his attributes intelligible, and endeavoring to make him less incomprehensible pull down the Deity to their weak intellect, they fall into miserable mistakes".
64. Op. cit., p. 215.
65. Op. cit., p. 239.
66. Mandeville ([1714–1729] 1924), vol. 2, p. 189. To clarify this, one can read the following passage: "Vinosity, so far as it is the effect of fermentation, is adventitious; and what none of the grapes could ever have received, whilst they remain single; and therefore, if you would compare the sociableness of Man to the vinosity of wine, you must shew me that in society there is an equivalent for fermentation" (op. cit., pp. 188–189). Mandeville thus saw in social relations the "equivalent" of fermentation.
67. Op. cit., p. 189.
68. As Dawkins wrote (1996, p. 92), "evolution never starts from a clean drawing board".
69. Mandeville ([1714–1729] 1924, vol. 2), pp. 287–288.
70. Op. cit., p. 132.
71. Op. cit., pp. 349–350.
72. Op. cit., p. 349. Mandeville (op. cit., vol. 1, p. 221) also stated: "the reciprocal services which all men pay to one another are the foundations of the society".
73. Op. cit., vol. 2, p. 349. This is the reason why Mandeville (op. cit., vol. 1, p. 344) also asserted that the "sociableness of man arises only from these two things, *viz.*

The Multiplicity of his desires, and the continual opposition he meets with in his endeavours to gratify them".

74. Op. cit., vol. 2, p. 284. As is well known, Adam Smith later insisted on the division of labour. Marx ([1867] 1976, vol. 1, p. 374, note 33) went as far as to say that Smith has "copied almost word for word" from Mandeville's text. It is in any case worth recalling that, concerning the division of labour, Weber ([1917] 1949, pp. 63–64) then stated that it is "the basic element in all those phenomena which we call, in the widest sense, *social-economic*". For his part, Mises ([1933] 1981a, p. 42) wrote that the division of labour is "the starting point" of social theory. Mandeville ([1714–1729] 1924, vol. 1, p. 356) was well aware of this: "[...] before a fine scarlet or crimson cloth can be produced, what multiplicity of trades and artificers must be employed! Not only such as are obvious, as wool-combers, spinners, the weaver, the cloth-worker, the scourer, the dyer, the setter, the drawer and the packer; but others that are more remote and might seem foreign to it; as the mill-wright, the pewterer and the chymist, which yet are all necessary as well as a greater number of other handicrafts to have the tools, utensils and other implements belonging to the trades already named."
75. This expression would later be used by Smith ([1776] 1976–83b, vol. 1, p. 27).
76. Social approval acts therefore as a curb on our passions. For it nourishes that *self-liking* which becomes the "cause" of self-respect (Mandeville, [1714–1729] 1924, vol. 2, pp. 129–131). As for the controlling function of religion, Mandeville argued in the *Fable* that "divine vengeance" and the oaths themselves are "of little service" without a "human power to enforce the obligation and punish the perjury" (op. cit., p. 268); he also stated that it is possible to consider a certain man an atheist only after he himself admits it (op. cit., p. 314); and he stated that "modern deism is no greater security than atheism" (ibid.). In his *Enquiry* (1732, pp. 23–24), however, he wrote that "the chief use" of religion consists of the "promises of allegiance and loyalty and all solemn engagement and asseverations, in which the invisible power [...] is invoked and appealed"; and he added that, "without a belief of an invisible cause, no man's word is to be relied upon".
77. Mandeville (1723), p. 253.
78. Hayek (1982), vol. 2, p. 109.
79. Mandeville ([1714–1729] 1924), vol. 1, p. 124.
80. Op. cit., p. 52.
81. Op. cit., p. 190.
82. Op. cit., p. 234.
83. Op. cit., p. 168.
84. Ibid.
85. Ibid.
86. Op. cit., p. 52.
87. Smith ([1759] 1976–83a), p. 308.
88. Viner (1937, p. 105, note 1).
89. Hayek (1978), p. 272. As Schatz (1907, pp. 60–61) pointed out, when it first appeared, *The Fable of the Bees* was denounced "as an attack on the Divine Majesty and the Royal Majesty" and considered capable of "drawing the plague onto the United Kingdom", so that more than "one pitiful soul believed that it was their duty to destroy such an abominable book".
90. Bayle ([1682] 1965–70a). vol. 3, p. 3.

91. Hayek (1978), p. 266. Magri (1987, p. xiii, note 15) stated that Hayek's is a "decisive" interpretation in understanding the thought of Mandeville (and of Hume and Smith). We will discuss the latter in the coming chapters.
92. Bayle ([1694] 1965–70b), p. 361.
93. The passage where these tones are strongest is the following: "As this prudent oeconomy, which some people call *saving*, is in private families the most certain method to increase an estate, so some imagine that whether a country be barren or fruitful, the same method, if generally pursued (which they think practicable) will have the same effect upon a whole nation, and that, for example, the *English* might be much richer than they are, if they would be frugal as some of their neighbours. This, I think, is an error" (Mandeville, [1714–1729] 1924, vol. 1, p. 182). As is well known, Mandeville's mercantilist tones received Keynes' approval (1936, pp. 359–362).
94. Schatz (1907), p. 60.
95. Kaye (1924), p. xcviii.
96. Mandeville's assertion ([1714–1729] 1924, vol. 1, p. 369) closes the first volume of the *Fable* and is repeated in the second volume (op. cit., vol. 2, p. 319). For his commentary, see Heckscher (1935, vol. 2, p. 293). The Swedish economist then reiterated the concept (op. cit., p. 319), arguing that the same idea had been expressed by Bacon "even a hundred years before".
97. Viner (1937), p. 99, note 87.
98. Viner's introduction is from 1953, later collected in Viner (1958, pp. 332–342); the quotation is taken from p. 341.
99. Ibid. It is clear that Heckscher and Viner did not take into account Mandeville's considerations about the impossibility of escaping the international division of labour. After focusing on internal cooperation, he wrote: " all these things are done at home and may be performed without extraordinary fatigue or danger; the most frightful prospect is left behind, when we reflect on the toil and hazard that are to be undergone abroad, the vast seas we are to go over, the different climates we are to endure, and the several nations we must be obliged for their assistance. *Spain* alone it is true might furnish us with wool to make the finest cloth; but what skill and pains, what experience and ingenuity are required to dye it of those beautiful colours. How widely are the drugs and other ingredients dispersed thro' the universe that are to meet in one kettle! Allum indeed we have of our own; argol we might have from the *Rhine*, and vitriol from Hungary; all this in Europe; but then for saltpetre in quantity we are forced to go as far as the *East-Indies*" (Mandeville, [1714–1729] 1924, vol. 1, pp. 356–357).
100. See Rosenberg (1963), Colletti (1975, pp. 287–289), Horne (1978, pp. 51–75), Scribano (1980, pp. 184–208), Simonazzi (2015) and the bibliographies provided in these texts.
101. Mandeville ([1714–1729] 1924), vol. 2, pp. 177–178. Unfortunately, the Mandevillian position was for a long time associated with that of Hobbes. Mandeville's explicit criticism of the author of the *Leviathan* was therefore not taken into account; and the fact that the two authors are on opposite positions has been overlooked, because one (Hobbes) was a supporter of an intentionally constructed order; and the other (Mandeville) opened the way to the understanding of the unintended order (Hayek, 1978, p. 257); cf. also Iannello (1998, pp. 120–125). This topic will be discussed further later (Chapter 3, Section 3.2).
102. Mandeville ([1714–1729] 1924), vol. 1, pp. 323–324. See also Cubeddu (2015) and the extensive bibliography indicated therein.

103. Mandeville ([1714–1729] 1924), vol. 2, p. 121.
104. Op. cit., pp. 182–183.
105. Kaye (1924), p. xcviii.
106. Infantino (2020a), pp. 18–32.
107. Hayek (1978), pp. 119–120.
108. Hayek (1960), p. 60.
109. It is significant that Quesnay ([1765] 1846, vol. 1, p. 48) wrote: "the laws which the Author of nature has instituted are just and perfect from the general point of view, when they conform to the order and the purposes which He has set Himself; for He Himself is the Author of the laws and the rules". Invited to Moscow by Catherine of Russia, to the sovereign's question about what constitutes the "science of government", Mercier de la Rivière replied: "To study the laws that God has so manifestly impressed on human society since the time of creation. To want to do more than this would be a great mistake and a disastrous undertaking" (Thiébault, 1860, vol. 3, pp. 167–168). This episode was also mentioned by Oncken (1902, vol. 1, pp. 421–422). For a critique of the conclusions reached by *laissez-faire*, see Cairnes (1873, p. 262).
110. Greig (1932), vol. 2, p. 205. As Schumpeter recalled (1954, p. 138, note 27), Morellet's "materials" were used in Jacques Peuchet's *Dictionnaire universel de la géographie commerçant*.
111. Schumpeter (1954), pp. 230–231.
112. Hayek (1982), vol. 1, p. 62.
113. Tocqueville (1856), p. 197. It is therefore worthwhile recalling that Mercier de la Rivière ([1767] 1846, vol. 2, pp. 536–537) affirmed the evident character of the essential order of every society; and he added that, as the evidence always has the same authority, it is not possible for the evidence of this order to be manifest and public without it governing despotically. Tocqueville (1856, p. 198) added: finding nothing that seems "conformable" to their ideal, "they went to the heart of Asia in search of a model. I do not exaggerate when I affirm that every one of them wrote in some place or other an emphatic eulogium on China. One is sure to find at least that in their books; and as China is very imperfectly known even in our day, their statements on its subject are generally pure nonsense."
114. Making use of a passage that Ortega y Gasset ([1930] 1946–83g, p. 177) wrote in another context, one could say that the innovation brought about by Mandeville's work "placed the average man – the great social mass – in conditions of life which are radically opposed to those that had always surrounded him. It turned public existence upside down [… and introduced] a new order, which has overturned the traditional one".

3. Francis Hutcheson and David Hume

> We have no evidence for such wisdom in the parts themselves as could have contrived their constitutions: and therefore must conclude that there is a superior *all-ruling Mind*. (Francis Hutcheson)
> When [philosophers speak as] priests and poets [...], I ask: who carried them into the celestial regions, who admitted them into the councils of the gods, who opened to them the book of fate [...]? (David Hume)

3.1　BETWEEN PAST AND FUTURE

As Leslie Stephen stated, "so long [...] as the older theological conception of the universe is unhesitatingly accepted, the only moral enquiry which is likely to flourish is casuistry, or discussions as to detail of that legal code whose origin and sanction are abundantly clear".[1] "Wider speculations as to morality inevitably occur as soon as the vision of God becomes faint".[2] The prohibition of murder is no longer pronounced by the deity. But the "sentiment of disapproval survives the clearly divine character of the prohibition";[3] and morality is identified with positive law. Hence the conclusion that evil is in that which is forbidden by the ruler; and good is in that which is permitted.[4] The compatibility of human actions is seen as the intentional product of the prescriptions of a single decision-maker.

It was not easy to free oneself from the idea that behind the compatibility of human actions there must always be an ordering mind. After so many years from Mandeville's work, James McCosh wrote:

> The author has [...] caught hold of a positive and important truth, the explanation of which carries us into some of the deepest mysteries of Providence, in which we see good springing out of vice, and God ruling this world in spite of its wickedness, and by means of its wickedness, but without identifying himself with it. [And yet] Mandeville was not able to solve the profound problem, and in dealing with it he uses expressions which look as if he intended to justify, or at least to palliate vice.[5]

It can be seen here that McCosh's attention focused on the "scandalous" part of Mandeville's work, but not on the most original and innovative portion.

For his part, Élie Halévy argued that in Mandeville there is a "natural identity of interests".[6] This is a complete misunderstanding: because, if there is a "natural identity of interests", the social order is already given. There is a Nature or a God who has acted and acts for us and who makes our actions compatible. Man is thus relieved of the problem. Order responds to an intentional and mysterious act of volition. This is exactly opposite to what Mandeville argues, because in his writings (as we have already highlighted) the compatibility of human actions is achieved through a process of permanent co-adaptation.

The first to take up Mandeville's legacy were the representatives of the Scottish Enlightenment. But the point requires several clarifications to be made. Sir William Hamilton identified Gershom Carmichael as the "real founder of the Scottish school of philosophy";[7] indeed, Carmichael was the first holder of the Chair of Moral Philosophy at Glasgow University. Subsequently, with a controversial choice, he was succeeded by Francis Hutcheson. And it is to the latter that McCosh attributed the credit for having expressed all the "characteristics of the school";[8] which is a judgement that has consolidated over time, so much to lead Hugh Trevor-Roper to consider the Irish philosopher as "the teacher of them all, the founder of the new Scottish philosophy".[9]

However, the important question is not to whom to give some kind of priority. It is to see how Carmichael and Hutcheson addressed the problem of the social order; and they both share the inability to free themselves from the idea that the compatibility of human actions is preordained by a divinity.[10] Which, from our point of view, is equivalent to saying that neither of them can be given any precedence. It was David Hume who took the path of unintended order. And while this, on the one hand, made him subject to Hutcheson's hostility, on the other it dug an unbridgeable fracture between two ways of conceiving individual and collective life.

3.2 HUTCHESON ON THE SHOULDERS OF SHAFTESBURY

It was Hutcheson himself who clearly manifested his cultural coordinates. In his book published in 1725 – *An Inquiry into the Original of our Ideas of Beauty and Virtue* – he stated in the subtitle that he wanted to explain and defend the *principles of the late Earl of Shaftesbury, against the author of the Fable of the Bees.* This statement already shows Hutcheson's debt towards Shaftesbury.[11] And it also suggests that, above all, he perceived Mandeville's work as a revival, in a different and more dangerous form, of the idea that underpins the Hobbesian system; and this is also confirmed by three letters against Mandeville, published the following year in the *Dublin Journal*.

We can therefore say that, whereas the target of Shaftesbury's polemics was Hobbes, Hutcheson was taking aim against the author of *The Fable of the Bees*. He acted as if Mandeville's criticism of Hobbes had never been formulated;[12] and this favoured the spread of an interpretation that, even many years later, posited that it was Mandeville who, "in his grimly humorous way, pointed to the enormous force of egoism in human affairs, and in effect dedicated for the theoretic solution of Hobbes".[13]

Hutcheson immediately made it clear that there exists a "universal benevolence";[14] and that this can be compared to the "principle of gravitation", which "extends to all bodys in the universe".[15] It "increases as the distance is diminished and is strongest when bodys come to touch each other".[16] This increase is "observable in the high degree" in the case of heroes and legislators, who benefit from "strong ties of friendship", "neighbourhood" and "partnership", which are "necessary to the order of human society".[17]

Faced with Mandeville's work, Hutcheson declared that *self-love* is "impossible";[18] and he asked himself: if we are devoid of "moral sense", can we appreciate men who love the public good?[19] To which he answered: "No, we could form no idea of such a temper";[20] we would consider them "hipocrites" and "rivals".[21] They could never induce us to admire the virtue or the virtues of others.[22] They would convey to us the idea of the advantages or disadvantages of actions.[23] And yet, "if we suppose that men have by nature a moral sense of goodness in actions, and that they are capable of disinterested love, all is easy".[24] If we have no moral sense, we cannot judge actions, but only consider them advantageous or disadvantageous; and we cannot honour or love those who act for the public good or have "any regard for their actions".[25] Without the "principle of benevolence", we can form a "metaphysical idea of publick good"; but we cannot wish anything extending beyond our "private interest".[26] Thus, virtue becomes

> the offspring of flattery, begot upon pride; that pride, in the bad meaning of the word, is the spurious brood of ignorance by our moral sense, and flattery only an engine, which the cunning may use to turn this moral sense in others, to the purposes of self-love in the flatterer.[27]

Hutcheson did not stop there. He also specified: "the old notions of natural affections, and kind instincts, the *sensus communis*, the *decorum*, and *honestum* are almost banished out of our books of morals; we must never hear of them in any of our lectures for fear of innate ideas: all must be interest, and some selfish view".[28] And he objected: "virtue itself, or good dispositions of mind are not directly taught, or produced by instruction";[29] "are the effect of the great Author of all things, who forms our nature for them".[30] More precisely, virtue consists "in love, gratitude, and submission to the deity, and in kind affections towards our fellows, and study of their greatest good".[31] And then, in an attempt to bolster his position, he did not hesitate to state: "all sects, except the Epicureans, owed that kind affections were natural to men; and that consulting the greatest public good of the whole, as it was the surest way for each individual to be happy so it was *secundum naturam o secundum rectam rationem*".[32]

Stephen rightly wrote that Hutcheson's theology "differs from Shaftesbury's", because he felt the need to attribute to the Creator "a slightly more distinct personality; the universal Parent is not so closely identified with nature".[33] This is why, in the inaugural lecture delivered in Glasgow in 1730, after praising the ethics of the "ancients" and recognizing that this had not been neglected by Richard Cumberland, Hutcheson added: "it was the excellent Lord Shaftesbury, a man combining nobility of mind with that of birth, who gave the best and most elegant account of this matter, although in other respects he is liable to censure from the theologians. And for my part I can assuredly not think of any objection to this".[34]

What is the issue? Shaftesbury had tried to erase the supernatural element of religion, retaining the divine element.[35] Which means that, in his system, "God is to be no longer a ruler, external to the world, but an immanental all-pervading force".[36] As a believer, Hutcheson could not have taken such a position; and, as a member of his world, he would not have been able to espouse it publicly. However, trying to provide consistency to the doctrines "which are in a state of solution in Shaftesbury's rather turbid eloquence", he made *moral sense* the "the keystone of an elaborate system".[37] He attributed to human beings a "faculty", of which, supposedly, they were originally bearers; as if to say that God created the conditions that make coexistence possible. Compatibility of actions was therefore pre-ordered. By means of a primal intervention, order was decided by the Divinity, to which Hutcheson repeatedly gave the name of "original Mind" or "original Being".

Can we in this way escape unintended consequences? It was Hutcheson himself who admitted that actions that seem to produce positive effects then generate negative results; and actions that seem to produce negative effects then generate positive results.[38] Not even the moral sense given to us by God can free us from the "paradox of consequences". This forced Hutcheson to take refuge in the justification that "no evil is allowed which is not necessary for superior good".[39] It follows that there is not only an order benevolently willed by God; there is also a destiny in the making, of which we do not know (and cannot know) anything, but which is very much present in the divine mind and which makes us suffer evil solely to give us a greater good. The promised goal is a guarantee of the justice of God.[40]

It is thus apparent that Mandeville's work belongs to a completely different territory, from which Hutcheson, without hiding his contempt, kept himself at a safe distance. He could at least have made some effort to try to grasp the dynamics of social cooperation proposed by Mandeville. Instead, he irrevocably cleaved to the position according to which, "if we have no other idea of good, but advantage to ourselves, every rational being must only act for its own advantage";[41] and he did not take any notice of the fact that every one of our actions intersects with that of others. Thus, he denied himself the possibility of grasping that what matters most in the intersubjective relationship is not the motivation of the actor, but what he needs to do in order to obtain from others the means he requires for the pursuit of his goals. In other words, he discarded what allows us to attain the conception of the social order where the actors, whatever their religious beliefs or worldviews, intentionally exchange means and unintentionally cooperate for the purposes of others. This means that the actors are not subject to a mandatory hierarchy of aims, because they operate with independent scales of priority.[42]

As well as Hobbes and Mandeville – quite incorrectly lumped together, as already mentioned – Hutcheson criticized Bayle, whose works he was very well acquainted with.[43] But he did not derive any benefit from a highly significant passage in the *Pensées diverses*, where Occam's presence is fully felt:

> The schools of theology, as well as those of philosophy, warn us not to multiply either beings or miracles without strict necessity, and thus authorize us to reject all assumptions that, even if not harmful, are devoid of any utility. According to this principle, one should never invoke miracles when things can be explained naturally and, if it appears to us to be completely useless and even contrary to the sanctity of the creator, one should not assume an extraordinary divine intervention in the production of an effect.[44]

3.3 HUME BETRAYED BY HUTCHESON

As is well known, the publication of the first two books of the *Treatise of Human Nature* was received coldly. With a mind to a possible academic career, Hume then asked Henry Home (later Lord Kames) to put him in touch with someone who could subject his work to a "serious perusal".[45] We do not know how things actually went. However, there is no doubt that Hume aspired to have Hutcheson's esteem and support. Which explains why he did not hesitate to send the manuscript of the third book of his *Treatise* to the Glasgow professor. The letter containing Hutcheson's comments has been lost. But Hume's response to it occupies an important place in the history of ideas.

After thanking his correspondent for his attention, the man who would later be known as *le bon David* wrote:

> what affected me most in your remarks is your observing that there wants a certain warmth in the cause of virtue, which, you think, all good men wou'd relish [...]. There are different ways of examining the mind as well as the body. One may consider it either as an anatomist or as a painter; either to discover its most secret springs and principles or to describe the grace and beauty of its actions. I imagine it impossible to conjoin these two views. Where you pull off the skin, and display all minute parts, there appears something trivial, even in the noblest attitudes and

most vigorous actions: nor can you render the object graceful or engaging but by cloathing the parts again with skin and flesh and presenting only their bare [...]. Any warm sentiments of morals, I am afraid, wou'd have the air of declamation amidst abstract reasonings, and wou'd be esteem'd contrary to good taste.[46]

In his *post scriptum* to the letter, Hume went on to state:

You are a great admirer of *Cicero* as well as I am. Please to review the 4th book *De finibus bonorum et malorum*, where you find him prove against the *Stoics* that, if there be no other goods but virtue, tis impossible there can be any virtue; because the mind wou'd then want all motives to begin its actions upon [...]. This proves that every virtuous action there must be a motive or impelling passion distinct from the virtue, and that virtue can never be the sole motive of any action.[47]

Now, considering these statements, which are already highly indicative of the distance that separated him from the Glasgow philosopher, one has to ask: which of the topics discussed led Hume to believe that he could obtain a hearing from Hutcheson? Hume was a tireless critic of ethical rationalism. At the very beginning of the third book of his *Treatise*, he made it clear that "the rules of morality [...] are not the conclusions of our reason".[48] This led to his disagreement with Locke. Locke had argued that he could place "morality among the science capable of demonstration"; and he had added that he did not doubt that "from self-evident propositions, by necessary consequences, as incontestable as those of mathematics, the measure of right and wrong might be made out".[49] Hume objected:

There has been an opinion very industriously propagated by certain philosophers that morality is susceptible of demonstration; and though no one has ever been able to advantage a single step in those demonstrations, yet it is taken for granted that this science may be brought to an equal certainty with geometry or algebra.[50]

Hume probably believed that his criticism of the idea of rationally building the rules of morality could win him Hutcheson's support. But the two thinkers proceeded from different premises and were aiming at equally different goals. This soon bore consequences.

Despite the polite and cordial nature of their relations, when the possibility of a chair of moral philosophy opened up at the University of Edinburgh, between 1744 and 1745, Hutcheson sided with those who opposed Hume's candidacy.[51] As William R. Scott wrote, Hutcheson encouraged Hume to pursue his research, but judged his possible influence as a university professor as "pernicious"; and he had no qualms in considering it his "duty" to warn the competent authorities against choosing Hume as "a teacher of morality".[52] In this case too, religious belief dominated Hutcheson's action.[53]

With his preface to the *System of Moral Philosophy*, which appeared posthumously in 1755, William Leechman was the first to give an account of Hutcheson's life and works;[54] but Leechman totally neglected what Hutcheson had critically written about *The Fable of the Bees*. The most frequently cited monograph on Hutcheson's life and work is Scott's. And yet Scott made scanty and inconsequential mention of the total rejection that the Irish philosopher had reserved for Mandeville's work.[55] Although he could have said more, Kaye went no further than a note on the subject in his fine edition of the *Fable*. He saw in Hutcheson "Mandeville's most persistent opponent";[56] he pointed out that the Glasgow philosopher was "one of the most famous of Shaftesbury's disciples";[57] but to this he added nothing. And Ernest C. Mossner, although he provided an extensive narration of the events that led to the rejection of Hume's candidacy, wrote that "Hutcheson presumably deemed Hume unfit for the chair as the University Senatus had imposed on holder [...] the duty of reconciling Moral philosophy with Divinity";[58] he did not even mention the possibility that what led Hutcheson to oppose the candidacy were Hume's intellectual debts towards Mandeville.

The fact is that, if we fail to remember that Hutcheson took advantage of every opportunity to "attack" *The Fable of the Bees*,[59] we deny ourselves the chance of grasping the reasons why even the slightest reference to Mandeville placed Hume in a situation of disadvantage: because he exhibited a cultural connection that Hutcheson, even without understanding its entire structure, fought against with all his strength.

Taking this into account, it is now possible to make additional comments on the aforementioned letter of September 1739. We have seen that with it Hume tried to defend his position by referring to Cicero. He claimed to have extracted from the fourth book of *De finibus bonorum et malorum* the idea that, "if there be no other goods without virtue, tis impossible there can be any virtue". Indeed, even if it were possible to find such an idea in that work, it remains that Cicero's writings point in another direction. Suffice it to think of what is asserted in *De officiis*. But Hume needed to find something that did not arouse suspicion, a source that Hutcheson could not judge with hostility (Epicurus, Lucretius, Bayle or Mandeville). And yet, despite the *ruse*, Hutcheson realized that behind Hume stood the presence of the author of *The Fable of the Bees*, who was in any case mentioned in the introduction to the *Treatise*.[60]

For the purposes of our discussion, we must not neglect that Hume saw in Mandeville something different from what Hutcheson saw. The latter's attention focused above all on the "provocative" statements contained in the reviled *Fable* and its prose commentary.[61] Hume side-stepped all this; he identified something new in Mandeville's work; namely, the "discovery" of society as *cosmos* or unintended order.[62] Which is equivalent to saying that behind social life and its institutions there is no human or divine *design*. In the mentioned letter of 1739, after having reproached Hutcheson for using a conception based on "final causes" (an argument judged "pretty uncertain and unphilosophical"), Hume had asked him the following questions: "For pray, what is the end of man? Is he created for happiness or for virtue? For this life or for the next? For himself or for his Maker?"[63] Obviously, Hutcheson could never accept that religious belief could lose its cogency and become a personal choice;[64] and he could not have accepted what derives from that.

3.4   HUME AND UNINTENDED ORDER

On page one of the third book of the *Treatise*, Hume wrote: "morality is a subject that interests us above all other; we fancy the peace of society to be at stake in every decision concerning it".[65] This means that the object of morality is the problem of social order. Hume energetically rejected the possibility of referring everything to the will of the Creator or some kind of invisible population of deities;[66] and at the same time rejected the idea of entrusting the compatibility of human actions to the prescriptions of the Leviathan or an earthly legislator. How then can one proceed?

Hutcheson believed that, if we look at "all nature as far as our knowledge extends", we can find the mechanism on which good is based;[67] and added that the "objections of the *Epicureans*, and of some *moderns*, arose from their ignorance".[68] Hume's outlook was quite different. He did not qualify others as ignorant. At the beginning of his *Treatise*, he already gave a negative judgement on the behaviour of those who boast of "their own systems" and discredit the work of others.[69] He remarked that "it is easy for one of judgment and learning to perceive the weak foundation, even of those systems which have obtained the greatest credit and have carried their pretensions highest to accurate and profound reasoning".[70] And he pointed out that "even the rabble without doors may judge from the noise and clamour which they hear that all goes not well within" the halls of science.[71] This is a direct consequence of the condition of ignorance and fallibility, to which we necessarily are subject, and which forces us, at every moment of our lives, to pay the price of our "blindness" and our "weakness".[72] What answer then can we give to the problem of social order?

The point the question stems from is the scarcity of available resources. If human beings "were supplied with everything in the same abundance", their mutual relations would not create any conflict or unexpected outcomes, "justice and injustice would be [...] unknown";[73] and this would also occur in the case where "*every one* had the same affection and tender regard for *every one* as for himself".[74]

This is not the case, however. Not unlike the "*state of nature*", the "*golden age*", "the most charming and the most peaceable condition that can possibly be imagined", is a "fiction" which "poets have invented".[75] And that is not all:

> Had every man sufficient *sagacity* to perceive, at all times, the strong interest which binds him to the observance of justice and equity, and *strength of mind* sufficient to persevere in a steady adherence to a general and a distant interest, in opposition to the allurements of present pleasure and advantage; there had never, in that case, been any such thing as government or political society, but each man, following his natural liberty, had lived in entire peace and harmony with all others.[76]

In other words, if human beings were omniscient, they would know exactly what to do and what not to do. Every question would cease to exist: social institutions themselves would be completely useless.[77]

Therefore, scarcity, ignorance and fallibility characterize our condition. "Man is altogether insufficient to support himself"; without relations with others, he "drops down into the deepest melancholy and despair".[78] Hence, the need to seek the cooperation of others. Even when not endowed with a "strong regard for public good", he must do so.[79] He "can form no wish which has not a reference to society".[80] "It is by society alone he is able to supply his defects."[81] "By society all his infirmities are compensated; and though in that situation his wants multiply every moment upon him, yet his abilities are still more augmented, all leave him in every respect more satisfied and happy than it is possible for him, in his savage and solitary condition, ever to become".[82]

When every individual person labours apart, and only for himself, his force is too small to execute any considerable work."[83] He expends his work to satisfy "all his different necessities", so that "he never attains a perfection in any particular art".[84] And, furthermore, the "least failure" in one of his activities "must be attended with inevitable ruin and misery".[85] "By the conjunction of forces, our power is augmented; by the partition of employments, our ability increases; and by mutual succour, we are less exposed to fortune and accidents."[86]

The foregoing clearly shows Hume's debt to Mandeville with regard to the division of labour. But what is most significant is that Hume embraced the idea that cooperation towards the purposes of others occurs on an unintentional basis.[87] The division of labour divides action into two parts: what each must personally do for themselves to achieve their own ends; and what they must do for others in exchange for their cooperation. What we do for others contributes, without any prior intentionality, to the realization of their goals; and what others do for us contributes, without their prior intentionality, to the attainment of our goals. Not surprisingly, with openly Mandevillian inspiration, Hume wrote: "If we examine the panegyrics that are commonly made of great men, we shall find that most of the qualities which are attributed to them may be divided into two kinds": those that are useful to those who act and those that allow a role to be played in society.[88]

This means that action is fuelled by our passions. And yet, since the attainment of our ends is made possible only by what others do for us, we must do what is asked of us by the other party in exchange for the cooperation they provide to us. Hence, the consequence that shirking one's obligations is tantamount to impairing the pursuit of one's goals or rendering them impossible, because fulfilment of obligations is the condition that allows each of us to benefit from the cooperation of others.[89]

The assessment of the usefulness of what we do must therefore not be based on the most direct outcomes. The failure to fulfil our obligations makes it immediately possible to obtain an advantage; and "men are always more concerned about the present life than the future".[90] But if this occurs, cooperation with the Other collapses. Which deprives us of the possibility of availing ourselves of the services of others. Thus, Hume wrote:

> After men have found by experience, that their selfishness and confined generosity [...] totally incapacitate them for society; and at the same time have observed that society is necessary to the satisfaction of those very passions, they are [...] induced to lay themselves under restraint of such rules as may render their commerce safe and commodious.[91]

The rules for living together are not a gift from benevolent nature.[92] They are the product of the impossibility of relinquishing the collaboration of others, of a process through which human minds become "mirrors to one another".[93] Like private property, they are moral relationships;[94] and it is they who make cooperation possible, because they co-adapt individual plans. Consequently, one can understand the reason why Hume was a tireless supporter of the *utility of rules* and an opponent of the *utility of acts*; and we can also understand the reason why he directed his preference to the "government of laws" rather than the "government of men".[95] For if the problem is that of the compatibility of actions, the general and abstract rule is that which, by delimiting the boundaries between actions, without imposing their contents, permits a social cooperation where each has their own scale of priorities: and need not subject themselves to a compulsory hierarchy of purposes. This is the situation where there is no need for a Great Legislator, that "mortall God" who with his unlimited power and the arbitrary character of his own prescriptions deprives us of our own freedom of choice.[96] Each can decide individually. One solely has to avoid encroaching on the other's sphere of autonomy.

It follows that the "rule of law" is the regulatory *habitat* of the unintended order. There no longer exists the "privileged point of view on the world"; and there is no one who embodies it and assumes the task of imposing his cogencies. Justice does not coincide with what we are enjoined to do. More precisely, since there is no mandatory hierarchy of ends, it is not possible to establish what is just; it is only possible to indicate what is unjust, or what the actors must not do.[97] From the relinquishment of the privileged source of knowledge and its prescriptions, we move to the "government of the law"; and we reach the unintended order, understood as a place of individual freedom of choice.

However, Hume did not restrict himself to explaining how it is possible to contribute unintentionally to the achievement of the goals of others. He focused on language and currency, which, like so many other institutions we benefit from, originated without the intervention of any sort of ordaining mind.[98] These are complex phenomena: they arise from extensive processes of interaction. And yet we never find ourselves confronted by unique and unrepeatable dynamics.[99] This does not occur in the realm of nature; and it does not occur in social life. If this were to happen, we would have to give up a great "variety of maxims", which "suppose a degree of uniformity and regularity".[100] We would no longer have science and the "relation of cause and effect" would remain "utterly unknown to mankind".[101] We would not be able to understand how to take advantage of unintended consequences of a positive character; and we would not know how to defend ourselves against unintended consequences of a negative character. We must therefore recognize that "we are placed in this world, where the true springs and causes of every event are entirely unknown to us".[102] However, if men "anatomise nature, according to the most probable, at least the most intelligible philosophy, they would find that these causes" and "all the events [...] about which they are so much concerned" are the effect of a "regular and constant machinery".[103]

3.5 RESEARCH TRADITIONS

As we have seen, Trevor-Roper identified Hutcheson as "the teacher of them all, the founder of the new Scottish philosophy". The considerations advanced so far show that there is an unbridgeable distance between the Glasgow philosopher and Hume. More precisely, they show that their thoughts stand on two opposing sides of culture. This also makes it impossible to accept the genealogy outlined by Trevor-Roper himself who, in addition to Hume, numbered among the descendants of Hutcheson, Adam Smith, William Robertson, Adam Ferguson and John Millar; and then went as far as to include the utilitarians of the nineteenth century.[104]

An advocate of an intentional order willed by God cannot be the progenitor of a family that made a decisive contribution to the theory of unintended order. In their fraught dialogue, Hutcheson and Hume were quick to exhibit a mutual estrangement, which in the case of the former became a total aversion. The forerunner of that family was Mandeville.[105] It was he who was responsible for the spectacular break with the conception of intentional order: both with the version that refers the compatibility of actions to divine will, and also the version that makes this compatibility descend from the prescriptions of some kind of Leviathan. Hence, the reversal of outlook which, by placing the "paradox of consequences" in a central position in the discussion, leads to the conclusion that the order established is not the product of any planning.

Hume fully grasped what Mandeville had undertaken. He made it his premise to reject any possible privileged source of knowledge. He saw the need to obtain the cooperation of others as what drives the co-adaptation of actions; and he identified the "rule of law" as the best tool to ensure the development of an extensive social process in which rules and institutions are subject to continuous change, because of the fact that choice trumps prescription. This fuels a social process that always remains unfinished, and which therefore has an ateleological character. That is why *le bon David* was considered a "precursor" of Charles Darwin.[106] More precisely, one can say that he was one of the "Darwinians before Darwin", the group of scholars who followed the path opened up by Mandeville in the domain of social phenomena.[107]

In addition to confirming that no link of kinship can be established between Hume and Hutcheson, this makes it possible to clearly mark out the boundaries with another tradition of research, that of utilitarianism in the strict sense.

Trevor-Roper was not content to make Hume and those who were inspired by him descend from Hutcheson. He also counted the nineteenth-century utilitarians among the epigones of the Glasgow philosopher. This makes it necessary to clarify at least two points. The first, and the most important, concerns the relationship between the evolutionary tradition and the more properly utilitarian tradition. The second concerns the compatibility of Hutcheson's philosophy with the idea, which is also found in his work, of the "greater and most extensive happiness".[108]

As for the first point, one should always bear in mind that the evolutionists were advocates of the utility of rules because, since they recognized the human condition of ignorance and fallibility, they saw the "rule of law" as the means that best allowed the exercise of individual freedom of choice, the exploration of the unknown, the correction of errors (the unintended consequences of a negative character) and the voluntary co-adaptation of individual plans. The utilitarians of the tradition linked to Jeremy Bentham were instead in favour of the "utility of acts". But the "frequent appeal to utility as the standard of action tends to introduce an uncertainty with respect to the conduct of other men",[109] since an action to which less utility is attributed is continuously substituted by others to which greater advantage is assigned; it allows "exceptions to the most important rules";[110] sanctions too charitably the use of "doubtful means" when a purpose has some attraction;[111] and enables "too great a latitude for discretion and policy in moral conduct".[112] As we already mentioned in the preface, it is here believed that the "relevant data" are available; and that the order that derives from them is a direct human creation.[113]

We can now examine the second point. Taken literally, Hutcheson's statement that we must aim for the "greatest and most extensive happiness" can be seen as a forerunner of Bentham's "felicific calculus". It represents the idea of a mathematical science of pleasure and pain. This clashes with the part of Hutcheson's work that most characterizes it. It pre-supposes a human rationality that the Glasgow philosopher himself denied. And it suggests the possibility that social order is built rationally. This is a hypothesis which is totally incompatible with Hutcheson's providentialist conception, which is based on innate moral sense, benevolence and virtue.

3.6 APPENDIX: JOSIAH TUCKER

Josiah Tucker wrote after Hume, but before Smith. He was one of the figures who was quickest to become aware of the impossibility of explaining human action without considering *self-love*; he realized that cooperation towards the ends of others can only occur unintentionally.

Hume held Tucker in great regard. He was sent some of his writings by Lord Kames, including *The Elements of Commerce, and Theory of Taxes*, published privately in Bristol in 1755. This is evidenced by a letter sent on 4 March 1758 to Kames himself, in which Hume thanked him; and judged that Tucker had a "profound knowledge of the theory of commerce, joined to an enlarged acquaintance with its practice".[114] On the same occasion, Hume also wrote:

> there is a hint thrown out in the papers, which gave me great satisfaction, because it concurs with a principle which I have thrown out to your Lordship, and which you seemed not to disapprove. I was indeed so pleased with it, that [...], as soon I should have occasion to give a new edition of my essays, I will make it a subject of treatment.[115]

And this he in fact did. The edition which Hume was referring to actually appeared that same year; and it contained the essay entitled *Of the Jealousy of Trade*, in which he extended the idea of the advantage of voluntary social cooperation to the international level.[116]

Born in Wales, Tucker was a member of the clergy (Dean of Gloucester). Considering it impossible to suppress *self-love*, he gave up the idea of being able to eliminate it or to weaken it.[117] He believed that one should "promote public interest by pursuing its own".[118] And he argued that, if the actor's personal reasons are prevented from bringing harm to his neighbour, the consequence is that "every individual (whether he intends it or not) will be promoting the good of his country, and of mankind in general, while he is pursuing his own private interest".[119]

Despite Hume's appreciation, Tucker's writings had no direct influence on the development of economic thinking.[120] None of his works were found in Smith's library, nor is he ever quoted in Smith's own writing. However, he exercised a significant "indirect influence", preparing British culture for a readier acceptance of the *Wealth of Nations*.[121]

NOTES

1. Stephen (1902), vol. 2, p. 2.
2. Ibid.
3. Ibid.
4. Op. cit., p. 5.
5. McCosh (1875), p. 56.
6. Halévy ([1901] 1972), p. 16.
7. McCosh (1875), p. 36.
8. Ibid.
9. Trevor-Roper (1967), p. 1639.
10. Obviously, this does not do away with the disagreement on other points. In the preface to his *Synopsis Theologiae Naturalis*, Carmichael (1729, pp. 9–12) argued with Hutcheson without naming him, objecting that *self-love* is not a reprehensible motive for action and adding that pursuing one's own interest does not discredit God or morality. See Mautner (1993), p. 68. We will see more clearly later that *self-love* and the pursuit of self-interest are Hutcheson's permanent polemical target.
11. As is well known, it was Robert Molesworth, who had had cordial contacts with Shaftesbury, who introduced Hutcheson to Shaftesbury's works. See McCosh (1875), p. 55.
12. For Mandeville's criticisms, see the previous discussion herein (Chapter 2, Section 2.4).
13. Robertson (1900), p. xxxix. The expression "grimly humorous way" testifies to what has already been reported in Chapter 2; namely, that the deliberately provocative part of the *Fable* has damaged the understanding and acceptance of Mandeville's work.
14. Hutcheson (1725a), p. 198.
15. Ibid.
16. Op. cit., p. 199.
17. Ibid.
18. Op. cit., p. 204.
19. Op. cit., p. 205.
20. Ibid.
21. Ibid.
22. Ibid.
23. Ibid.
24. Ibid.
25. Op. cit., pp. 205–206.
26. Op. cit., p. 206.

27. Ibid.
28. Hutcheson (1750), p. 7.
29. Hutcheson (1725a), p. 253.
30. Ibid.
31. Hutcheson (1750), p. 53.
32. Ibid.
33. Stephen (1902), vol. 2, p. 57.
34. Hutcheson (1730), p. 136.
35. Stephen (1902), vol. 2, p. 27.
36. Ibid.
37. Op. cit., p. 57. Obviously, the "natural tendency to virtue" conflicts with the "dogma of human corruption" (op. cit., p. 29). Which makes "revelation superfluous" and gives "support to deism" (Mautner, 1993, p. 66). Herein lies the reason why critics have never neglected Hutcheson's link with Shaftesbury's work (op. cit., pp. 66–84). It is a link that always comes to the surface. As is well known, Shaftesbury himself had asserted that there is no virtue in those who do good in the hope of receiving a reward or for fear of punishment (Shaftesbury, [1711] 1900, vol. 2, p. 267). And Hutcheson (1725b, p. 103) argued that true virtue or benevolence is enacted without thinking about future rewards or punishments, although he then said that considerations "of rewards and punishments are useless" and that they are the only means to keep "the selfish passions" at bay. Furthermore, in his *System of Moral Philosophy*, Hutcheson did not hesitate to exalt nature in a manner not dissimilar to Shaftesbury's (Hutcheson, 1755, pp. 169–170).
38. Hutcheson (1725a, p. 161) had to recognize that an action deemed fit to pursue a certain end may actually achieve a different one. And he was forced to admit that "many actions" can produce results exactly opposite to those planned (op. cit., pp. 164–165).
39. Hutcheson (1755), p. 198.
40. With the words of Hume ([1748] 1902a, p. 138), which have already been highlighted in Chapter 1, one could say that in Hutcheson there is "all the fruitless industry to account for the ill appearances of nature [and life] and save the honour of the gods; while we must recognize the reality of that evil and disorder, with which the world so much abounds".
41. Hutcheson (1725a), p. 138.
42. Had Hutcheson understood this, the expression "the good of the whole", which pre-supposes a higher hierarchy of aims and excludes the possibility of independent priority scales, would not have appeared so often in his pages. This is exactly the collectivist vision demolished by Mandeville and those who followed his pioneering work.
43. Hutcheson had also repeatedly addressed his criticisms against Epicurus; and he did not spare Lucretius either (see Hutcheson, 1755, p. 111).
44. Bayle ([1682] 1965–70a), p. 137.
45. Letter of 13 February 1739, in Greig (1932), vol. 1, p. 26. See also Scott (1900), p. 116 and Mossner (2001), p. 134.
46. Letter of 17 September 1739, in Greig (1932) vol. 1, pp. 32–33. The metaphor of the anatomist and the painter can also be found on the last page of the *Treatise*. See Hume ([1739–1740] 1930), vol. 2, p. 312.
47. Greig (1932), vol. 1, p. 35.
48. Hume ([1739–1740] 1930), vol. 2, p. 167.

49. Locke ([1690] 1924), p. 277.
50. Hume ([1739–1740] 1930), vol. 2, p. 172. On this point, see Raphael (1974), pp. 14–29.
51. This disappointed Hume's expectations. Suffice it to say that even in the well-known *Letter from a Gentleman to his Friend in Edinburgh*, with which he tried to defend himself from the accusation of being an enemy of religion and morality, levelled against him by most of the Presbyterian clergy and, in particular, by the Reverend William Wishart, Principal of the University of Edinburgh, Hume declared that he agreed "with all the antient moralists, as well as with Mr. *Hutcheson*, professor of Moral Philosophy in the University of Glasgow" (Hume, [1745] 1967, p. 30).
52. Scott (1900), p. 128. See also Mossner (2001), pp. 153–158. As is well known, Hume tried to obtain the university chair a second time. This was in 1751, at Glasgow University. But on that occasion too his candidacy was rejected.
53. Scott (1900), p. 21.
54. Leechman (1755), pp. i–xlviii.
55. Scott (1900), p. 35.
56. Mandeville ([1714–1729] 1924), vol. 2, p. 345, note 1.
57. Ibid.
58. Mossner (2001), p. 157.
59. Hayek (1978), p. 252. It is therefore not enough to argue that Hutcheson and Mandeville had different anthropological conceptions (see indicatively Norton, 1982, pp. 60–61). One must emphasize the former's clear hostility towards the latter.
60. Hume ([1739–1740] 1930), vol. 1, p. 6, note 1.
61. Hutcheson (1750, p. 67) wrote: "Thus we may see with how little reason vices are either counted necessary, or actually subservient to the public happiness, even in our present corruption."
62. It is no surprise that Hayek (1978, p. 264) also argued that Hume's work has the merit of shedding light on the "significance" of Mandeville's work.
63. Greig (1932), vol. 1, p. 33. Moreover, in the introduction to his *Treatise*, Hume wrote: "any hypothesis, that pretends to discover the ultimate original qualities of human nature, ought at first to be rejected as presumptuous and chimerical" (Hume, [1739–1740] 1930, vol. 1, p. 6).
64. This is directly borne out by the letter Hutcheson sent to Henry Home in April 1739, in which the Glasgow philosopher complained about the length of the *Treatise*, which for this reason he had not finished reading, and showed impatience with Hume's attitude towards religion (see Ross, 1966, pp. 69–72). This means that, even without taking into account the questions posed to him in Hume's letter, the theory of causation expounded in the first book of the *Treatise* had already alarmed Hutcheson. On the consequences of this theory on the religious level, cf. McCosh (1875), pp. 145–147.
65. Hume ([1739–1740] 1930), vol. 2, p. 165.
66. Hume ([1757] 1889, pp. 10–12) did not shut his eyes to anything in the human condition: "We are placed in this world, where the true springs and causes of every event are entirely unknown to us; nor have we either sufficient wisdom to foresee, or power to prevent, those ills with which we are continually threatened. We hang in perpetual suspence between life and death, health and sickness, plenty and want, which are distributed amongst the human species by secret and unknown causes, whose operation is often unexpected, and always unaccounta-

ble [...]. No wonder, then, that mankind, being placed in such an absolute ignorance of causes, and being at the same time so anxious concerning their future, should immediately acknowledge a dependance on invisible powers possessed of sentiment and intelligence [...]. Nor is it long before we ascribe to them thought. And reason, and passion, and sometimes even the limbs and figures of men, in order to bring them nearer to a resemblance with ourselves." And yet, as we have reported in the epigraph of this chapter, referring to the philosophers who say the same things as "priests and poets", Hume ([1748] 1902a, p. 138) polemically asked: "who carried them into the celestial regions, who admitted them into the councils of the gods, who opened to them the book of fate?".

67. Hutcheson (1755), p. 180.
68. Ibid.
69. Hume ([1739–1740] 1930), vol. 1, p. 3.
70. Ibid.
71. Ibid.
72. Hume ([1748] 1902a), p. 31.
73. Hume ([1739–1740] 1930), vol. 2, p. 200. It follows that private property is a product of scarcity. By marking out the boundaries between what belongs to each one, it performs the function of regulating conflicts. This is why Hume (op. cit., pp. 199–200) wrote: "The selfishness of men is animated by the few possessions we have, in proportion to our wants; and it is to restrain this selfishness, that men have been obliged to separate themselves from the community, and to distinguish betwixt their own goods and those of others."
74. Ibid.
75. Op. cit., p. 198. See also Hume ([1751] 1902b), p. 189.
76. Hume ([1751] 1902b), p. 205.
77. See the corresponding text in note 96 of Chapter 1.
78. Hume ([1739–1740] 1930), vol. 2, p. 72.
79. Op. cit., p. 230.
80. Op. cit., p. 81.
81. Op. cit., p. 191.
82. Ibid.
83. Ibid.
84. Ibid.
85. Ibid.
86. Op. cit., pp. 191–192.
87. The system of cooperation itself originated from the consideration of the interests of the actors, but not from the assessment of the social advantages: those who adopted it did not have that as their purpose (Hume, [1739–1740] 1930, vol. 2, p. 231; [1742–1757] 1903, p. 269). It should be added that the theory of unintended consequences is found throughout Hume's entire oeuvre. Obviously, it was used in support of free trade: "Our Jealousy and our hatred of France are without bounds [...]. These passions have occasioned innumerable barriers and obstructions upon commerce [...]. But what have we gained by the bargain? We lost the French market for our woollen manufactures and transferred the commerce of wine to Spain and Portugal, where we buy worse liquor at a higher price. There are few Englishmen who would not think their country absolutely ruined, were French wines sold in England so cheap and in such abundance as to supplant, in some measure, all ale and home-brewed liquors: but would we lay aside our prejudice, it would not be difficult to prove, that nothing could be more

innocent, perhaps advantageous" (Hume, [1742–1757] 1903, pp. 322–323). In other words, protectionism seems to ensure advantages and cause disadvantages; and free trade seems to produce disadvantages and generate advantages.

88. Hume ([1739–1740] 1930), vol. 2, p. 282.
89. Op. cit., p. 236. See also Hume ([1751] 1902b), pp. 218–219.
90. Hume ([1739–1740] 1930), vol. 2, p. 227; see also p. 239 and p. 269.
91. Op. cit., p. 203.
92. Op. cit., pp. 183–190.
93. Op. cit., p. 82.
94. Op. cit., p. 196: "A man's property is some object related to him. This relation is not natural, but moral, founded on justice."
95. Hume ([1742–1757] 1903), p. 95.
96. It is significant that Hume ([1739–1740] 1930, vol. 2, p. 201) stated that "a single act of justice is frequently contrary to *public interest*"; see also Hume ([1751] 1902b), p. 305. Moreover, read the following passage: "And in the event it has hitherto been found, that, though some sensible inconveniences arise from the maxim of adhering strictly to law, yet the advantages overbalance them, and should render the English grateful to the memory of their ancestors, who, after repeated contests, at last established that noble [...] principle" (Hume, [1754–1761] 1983, vol. 5, pp. 329–330). The expression "mortall God" is Hobbes' ([1651] 1914, p. 89).
97. Hayek (1969, p. 120) wrote that Hume: "with his profound conviction of the imperfection of all human reason and knowledge, did not expect much positive good from political organization. He knew that the greatest political goods, peace, liberty and justice, were in their essence negative, a protection against injury rather than positive gifts. No man strove more ardently for peace, liberty and justice. But Hume clearly saw that the further ambitions which wanted to establish some other positive justice on earth were a threat to those values."
98. Hume ([1739–1740] 1930), vol. 2, p. 196; ([1751] 1902b), p. 306.
99. Hume ([1748] 1902a), p. 82.
100. Op. cit., p. 85.
101. Op. cit., p. 82.
102. See previous note 66.
103. Hume ([1757] 1889), pp. 10–11.
104. Trevor-Roper (1967), pp. 1639–1640.
105. Hayek (1988), p. 284.
106. See Bay (1968), p. 33. Making use of a few excerpts from the *Dialogues on Natural Religion*, Hayek (1969, pp. 226–227) argued that Hume was "clearly aware that the same argument [used in the social sphere] could also be used to explain the evolution of biological organisms". First: "may matter be susceptible of many and great revolutions, through the endless periods of eternal duration", and the "incessant changes, to which every part of it is subject, seem to intimate some such general transformations" (Hume, [1779] 1907, p. 89). Subsequently: "No form, you say, can subsist, unless it possess those powers and organs, requisite for its subsistence: some new order or economy must be tried, and so on, without intermission; till at last some order, which can support and maintain itself, is fallen upon" (op. cit., p. 110). Further: "A perpetual war is kindled among all living creatures" (op. cit., p. 126). Hayek (1969, p. 119) wrote that "the transmission of ideas from Hume to Darwin is continuous and can be traced in detail"; and added: "The most direct channel seems to have been Erasmus

Darwin, who was clearly influenced by Hume and whose influence on his grandson is unquestioned" (op. cit., note 53). In this regard, it is not out of place to recall the period of study spent by Erasmus in Edinburgh (Darwin Ch., [1879] 2003, pp. 22–23); see also King-Hele (1985, p. 170).
107. It was Pollock (1908, p. 42) who defined Montesquieu, Burke and Savigny as "Darwinians before Darwin". Mandeville, Hume and, as we shall see, Smith deserve this name even more.
108. Hutcheson (1725a), p. 165.
109. Stewart ([1828] 1859), p. 184.
110. Ibid.
111. Ibid.
112. Ibid.
113. As Halévy ([1901] 1972, p. 506) wrote, in utilitarianism in the strict sense, "it is the benevolence and the competence of the legislator that is counted on to establish [... the compatibility of actions], by means of limitations imposed on individual liberties". As we shall see, even greater is the distance between the cultural tradition of Mandeville, Hume, Smith and the French positivist sociology, represented by Auguste Comte and his followers, in which the idea of the social order as an unintended product of intentional human actions becomes inconceivable. See Chapter 5, Section 5.3.
114. Greig (1932), vol. 1, pp. 270–271.
115. Op. cit., p. 272.
116. Hume's letter to Lord Kames ended with the following passage: the "narrow spirit of nations, as well as individuals, ought carefully to be repressed; and I am glad to find that Mr. Tucker is likely to employ his talents and abilities in so useful a manner" (ibid.).
117. Tucker (1755), p. 7.
118. Ibid.
119. Op. cit., p. 9.
120. Clark (1903), p. 225. Apart from Hume, the only scholar of the time to be interested in Tucker was Turgot, whose first work was the French translation of Tucker's *Reflections on the Expediency of a Law for the Naturalisation of Foreign Protestants* (see Schumpeter, 1954, p. 226). As can be seen from a letter of his dated 16 June 1768, Hume was the link between Tucker and Turgot (Greig, 1932, vol. 2, pp. 179–181).
121. Clark (1903), p. 226.

4. Charles-Louis de Montesquieu and Adam Smith

> The laws of Minos, Lycurgus and Plato presuppose a singular mutual surveillance of all citizens, very difficult to ensure amid the confusion, negligence and vastness of the affairs of a great people. (Charles-Louis de Montesquieu)
>
> Benevolence may, perhaps, be the sole principle of action in the Deity [...], so imperfect a creature as man, the support of whose existence requires so many things external to him, must often act from many, other motives. (Adam Smith)

4.1 MONTESQUIEU AND THE VARIABILITY OF MODELS OF LIFE

Montesquieu's gnoseological assumptions are no different from those of Mandeville and Hume.[1] His actor is "a limited being, subject to ignorance and error".[2] Knowledge of time and place is dispersed within society, so much so that about all facts we "can have better information in a public forum than a monarch in his palace".[3] A king is not capable of "conducting an intricate affair, of seizing and improving the opportunity and critical moment of action".[4] And politics, understood in the Machiavellian view as "the science of cunning and artifice", harms justice, because each of its acts produces a sequence of unpredictable outcomes.[5]

As for rules and institutions, they are a product of social interaction. They cannot be considered as unique and permanent answers to the problem of living together; they are subject to all the variability imposed by the historical-social context and human fallibility.[6] Montesquieu found confirmation of this in his travels, in his stay in England, in his long pilgrimage through the pages of history, in his study of the work of the British diplomat Paul Rycaut on the Ottoman Empire, in his reading of the accounts of the great travellers, such as Jean-Baptiste Tavernier, François Bernier and Jean Chardin.[7] It is an established fact that, starting with his *Lettres persanes*, the variability of models of life was the issue to which he drew attention. Not surprisingly, in his dialogue with Ibben, Rica noted: "We tread, indeed, the same earth; but it seems incredible, remembering in the presence of the men of this country those of the country in which you are";[8] here there is a "magician who is called Pope": "he makes believe that three are no more than one; that the bread which he eats is not bread; the wine which he drinks is not wine; and a thousand things of a like nature";[9] here "a piece of paper is coin".[10]

This begs the question of why models of life are so different from country to country. Unfortunately, we no longer have the text of the *Traité général des devoirs de l'homme*. At the beginning of the account that Jean-Jacques Bel gave of it, we read the following statement: "Those who said that blind fate produced all the effects that we see in the world, said a great absurdity."[11] Montesquieu's objective was to identify what lies behind social phenomena. In other words, he went in search of "general causes, [...] which operated in every [...] society, and either raise and maintain it, or else involve it in ruin";[12] and was guided by the idea that "all accidental conjunctures are subordinate to these causes", with the consequence that, if "a particular cause has been destructive of a state, some general cause presided, and made a single battle be the inevitable ruin of that state".[13]

Montesquieu went on to write of himself:

> I have first of all considered mankind; and the result of my thoughts has been, that amidst such an infinite diversity of laws and manners, they were not solely conducted by the caprice of fancy. I have laid down the first principles, and have found that the particular cases follow from them; that the histories of all nations are only consequences of them; and that every particular law is connected with another law, or depends on some other of a more general extent.[14]

One can thus understand the reason why Rica also told Usbek:

> With us, character is uniform, because it is constrained; we do not see people as they are, but as they are forced to be; in that slavery of heart and mind, it is only fear that utters a dull routine of words, very different from the language of nature which expresses itself so variously. Dissimulation, that art so practised and so necessary with us, is here unknown: they say everything, see everything, and hear everything; hearts are as open as faces; in manners, in virtue, even in vice, one detects always a certain artlessness.[15]

And so (Usbek asks Ibben): "We are astonished that there is hardly ever any change in the government of eastern princes: how could it be otherwise, when we bear in mind their terrible tyranny?"[16] The government of "one man" is always inadequate and dangerous.

> Augustus (for that was the name offered by flattery to Octavius) was careful to establish order, or rather a durable servitude; for when once the sovereignty has been usurped in a free state, every transaction on which an unlimited authority can be founded, is called a regulation; and all instances of disorder, commotion, and bad government, are represented as the only expedients to preserve the just liberty of the subject.[17]

In other words, when "there be only the momentary and capricious will of a single person to govern the state, nothing can be fixed, and of course there is no fundamental law".[18] The "rule of men" prevails.

It follows that the institutionalization of social change and the extension of public power stand in an inverse relationship. Observed from a gnoseological point of view, this means that a system that prevents individual freedom of choice, and therefore the institutionalization of change, makes a process of systematic correction of errors impossible. That is why the "wisest" government is the one in which "there is a body which examines it perpetually and is perpetually examining itself".[19] In this case, "its errors are of such a nature, as never to be lasting, and are frequently useful" for the spirit of attention they infuse in the nation.[20] It is the same situation that makes it possible to develop trade. This bears with it "frugality, economy, moderation, labour, prudence, tranquility, order, and rule".[21] "Commerce is a cure for the most destructive prejudices": "it is almost a general rule, that wherever we find agreeable manners, there commerce flourishes; and that wherever there is commerce, there we meet with agreeable manners".[22] The idea that commercial activities and luxury can corrupt costumes is simply "le plainte de Platon".[23]

Consistently with his understanding of the social process, Montesquieu opposed contractualist theories, not unlike Mandeville and Hume. Consequently, he rejected the idea that there may be a beginning of society. For Usbek wrote to Rhedi:

> I have never heard public law discussed, without a preliminary careful inquiry into the origin of society, which seems to me absurd. If men did not unite, if they avoided and fled from each other, it would be necessary to ask the reason, and to inquire why they kept apart; but we are all born with relations.[24]

There is an awareness here that human beings are what they are as a result of social cooperation, which is a positive-sum game. Usbek himself (in the apology of the Troglodytes) said:

> They loved their wives and were beloved most tenderly. Their utmost care was given to the virtuous training of their children. They kept before their young minds the misfortunes of their countrymen and held them up as a most melancholy example. Above all, they led them to see that the interest of the individual was bound up in that of the community; that to isolate oneself was to court ruin [...]; and that in acting justly by others, we bestow blessings on ourselves.[25]

Interest is therefore "the greatest monarch in the world".[26]

4.2 MONTESQUIEU BETWEEN THE MYTH OF SPARTA AND THE GREAT SOCIETY

What we have set out so far suggests that in Montesquieu's reflections there are no concessions to the idea of intentional order. But that is not the case. Both in the *Traité général des devoirs de l'homme* and in the *Esprit des lois*, the statement that it was not a "blind fatality" that determined "the various effects we behold in this world" (because that would be a "great absurdity") is accompanied by the idea that, if it had been a "fatality", there would not have been "intelligent beings".[27] In the *Esprit des lois*, Montesquieu went on to write:

> God is related to the universe, as Creator and Preserver; the laws by which He created all things are those by which He preserves them. He acts according to these rules, because He knows them; He knows them, because He made them; and He made them, because they are in relation to His wisdom and power.[28]

And, perhaps to temper the meaning of these words, he added: "the creation, which seems an arbitrary act, supposes laws as invariable as those of the fatality of the Atheists".[29] This caused him, as is well known, to be accused of atheism, to which Montesquieu replied, recalling, among other things, that he argued that man, "a finite nature, and consequently liable to error", may forget "his Creator", but is immediately recalled to himself.[30]

This is not all. As we have seen, Montesquieu stated, in his *Lettres persanes*, that "interest is the greatest monarch in the world". But in that same text, in the apology of the Troglodyte, after having asserted that "the interest of the individual" is always "bound up with that of the community", he wrote that "the cost of virtue should never be counted, nor the practice of it regarded as troublesome".[31] In the *Esprit des lois*, discussing political regimes, he went on to state:

> I have already observed that it is the nature of a republican government, that either the collective body of the people, or particular families, should be possessed of the supreme power; of a monarchy, that the prince should have this power, but in the execution of it should be directed by established laws; of a despotic government, that a single person should rule according to his own will and caprice.[32]

Let us leave the situation of monarchies till last. In regard to republics, Montesquieu pointed out that "the politic Greeks, who lived under a popular government, knew no other support than virtue",[33] and added that everyone, "to be a virtuous man, must intend to be one, and love the State for itself".[34] The motivation of the actors must therefore coincide with the social justification. In other words, republican regimes bring about an order of an intentional type, based on the virtue of the citizens. As for despotic government, it is based on "fear".[35] The despot "is directed by no rule, and his own caprices are subversive of all others".[36] "The Grand Seignior was not obliged to keep his word, or oath, when he limited thereby his authority".[37] There is no doubt that here too we are dealing with an order that is established intentionally.

We can now consider "monarchical government". In this case, "the state subsists independently of the love of our country, of the thirst for true glory, of self-denial, of the sacrifice of our dearest interests, and of all those heroic virtues which we admire in the ancients".[38]

> What is going on here? The laws supply the place of those virtues; [...] the state dispenses with them [...]. Though all crimes be in their own nature public, yet there is a distinction between crimes really public and those that are private, which are so called because they are more injurious to individuals than to the community.[39]

This is nothing less than an exposition of what happens under the "rule of law". The law delimits the boundaries between actions; and the resulting order is unintended. The reference is clearly directed to English institutions, to which Montesquieu accorded his preference.[40] But he added something else. While stressing that "virtuous princes are so very rare" and mentioning "the wretched character of courtiers", he stated that honour prevails. "Honour sets all the parts of the body politic in motion, and by its very action connects them; thus, each individual advances the public good, while he only thinks of promoting his own interest".[41] Therefore, we find ourselves faced with two explanations, and both make use of the idea of unintended consequences. Being well aware that "virtuous princes" are rare and knowing "the wretched character of courtiers", Montesquieu could have avoided to resort to honour, on which the second explanation hinges, and where the actors do not pursue their own interests, but only *believe* that they are pursuing them.

But there is more. What was argued in respect of the republican regime requires specific analysis. Montesquieu wrote that in the "Greek republics" it was considered that "citizens" should not devote themselves "to trade, to agriculture, or to the arts";[42] he praised Sparta, its "grandeur" and its "glory";[43] and attributed to it "so infallible" institutions "that it signified nothing to gain a victory over that republic without subverting her polity".[44] This is the reason why Elizabeth Rawson, after having commented that the second part of the eighteenth century was "the great age of modern Laconomania", saw Montesquieu himself as the person who established the conditions for the rebirth of the myth of Spartan society.[45] It is here not surprising that, shortly after the publication of the *Esprit des lois*, Jean-Jacques Rousseau defined Sparta as a "Republic of demi-Gods rather than of men";[46] and he was not alone. The list of thinkers or mere political activists who fuelled "Laconomania" is long.[47] But what is most important is that Louis de Jaucourt, in the *Encyclopédie*, in writing the entry for *Lacédémone* (*Republique de*), recruited the authority of Montesquieu and considered Sparta a "marvellous republic", "terror of the Persians" and "admiration of the Greeks".[48] It was created in this way the illusion that freedom can be born from imperatively imposed *virtue*. It is the mirage of a world in which social justification coincides with the motivation of the actor.[49]

If Montesquieu had dwelt on the types of social cooperation, he could have offered the reader a more consistent account. Mandeville and Hume had focused on the division of labour. And they had understood that it may be voluntary or enforced.[50] The former case gives rise to a compatibility of actions of an unintended character, because it is underpinned by individual freedom of choice and the "rule of law"; the latter imposes a mandatory hierarchy of ends. This means that Montesquieu should have given a wider extent to what he himself had claimed; namely, that institutions have a "very great relation to the manner in which the several nations procure their subsistence".[51] This would have shown precisely that men make a living through voluntary or coercive cooperation.

However, Montesquieu realized that he had placed himself in a Procrustes bed. He was therefore forced to acknowledge that "in Greece there were two sorts of republics: the one military, like Sparta; the other commercial, as Athens".[52] We know that the former was like "a military encampment", where no one was allowed to live according to their choices;[53] foreigners were banished; and no merchant ships landed in its ports.[54] The other was open to the world.[55] Consequently, it is not possible to equate all the ancient republics. As for the situation of his own time, Montesquieu himself had to admit that contemporary politicians did not speak of virtue, but were "entirely taken up with manufacture, commerce, finances, opulence, and luxury":[56] a glaring break with the conceptions prevalent in the ancient world.[57] Hence the inapplicability of the teachings "of Minos, of Lycurgus, and of Plato", based on the assumption of being able to achieve a "singular mutual surveillance of all citizens, very difficult to ensure amid the confusion, negligence and vastness of the affairs of a large people".[58] The answer cannot be provided by the "government of a single man".[59] Compatibility of actions cannot be intentionally determined by a single ordering mind. "In great societies, the multiplicity, variety, embarrassment, and importance of affairs, as well as the facility of purchasing, and the slowness of exchange, require" a different solution:[60] one which prevents the "same man or the same body, whether of the nobles or of the people, to exercise those three powers, that of enacting laws, that of executing the public resolutions, and of trying the causes of individuals".[61] There no longer is the single decision-maker who, by imposing a mandatory hierarchy of ends, prescribes the contents of actions and is the sole judge of all behaviour. What prevails is the general and abstract rule, which guarantees each person's areas of autonomy, that is to say freedom of choice.[62]

4.3 SMITH AND THE BIRTH OF SOCIAL NORMS

As Rawson wrote, "with the victory of Adam Smith's doctrines, foreshadowed by Hume, the idea that Sparta was, as a society, peculiar and irrelevant, [...] gained authority".[63] Smith knew that legislators like Solon had encouraged "trade and commerce and obliged every one" to get their children to commit themselves to learn "some trade";[64] and he knew that "at Sparta there were no trades at all".[65]

But this was preceded by a deeper concern. We cannot exactly pinpoint the period in which the essay on the *History of Astronomy* was written. But there is a phrase in Smith that helps us out. He stated that Newton's "followers", "from his principles, ventured even to predict the returns of several [... comets], particularly of one which is to make its appearance in 1758".[66] This means that the text was written before that date.

The *History of Astronomy* therefore precedes in order of time Smith's great works;[67] and it is here that Smith first used the expression "invisible hand". Wishing to refer to that "vulgar superstition which ascribes all the irregular events of nature to the favour or displeasure of intelligent, though invisible beings, to gods, daemons, witches, genii, fairies",[68] he spoke, to be accurate, of the "invisible hand of Jupiter".[69] And he added:

> it may be observed, that in all Polytheistic religions, among savages, as well as in the early ages of Heathen antiquity, it is the irregular events of nature only that are ascribed to the agency and power of their gods. Fire burns, and water refreshes; heavy bodies descend, and lighter substances fly upwards, by necessity of their own nature; nor was the invisible hand of Jupiter ever apprehended to be employed in those matters.[70]

And yet "thunder and lightning, storms and sunshine, those more irregular events, were ascribed to his favour, or his anger".[71] It is believed that "other intelligent beings, whom they imagined, but knew not, were [...] supposed to act in the same manner; not to employ themselves in supporting the ordinary course of things [..., but] to stop, to thwart, and to disturb it".[72] It was thus that "in the first ages of the world, the lowest and most pusillanimous superstition supplied the place of philosophy".[73]

Smith made the problem he was measuring even clearer:

> In the first ages of the world, the seeming incoherence of the appearances of nature, so confounded mankind, that they despaired of discovering in her operations any regular system. Their ignorance, and confusion of thought, necessarily gave birth

to that pusillanimous superstition, which ascribes almost every *unexpected event*, to the arbitrary will of some designing, though invisible beings, who produced it for some private and particular purpose.[74]

In other words, every unexpected phenomenon is considered to be the intentional product of some actor, even if an imaginary one.[75]

In a letter sent to Hume on 16 April 1773, Smith defined the *History of Astronomy* as "a fragment of an intended juvenile work", which had remained unfinished.[76] It shows that the author had thought of entrusting science with the task of explaining the "unexpected events" that occur in the field of nature. And yet the works for which Smith is remembered, the *Theory of Moral Sentiments* and the *Wealth of Nations*, are devoted to a systematic investigation of social phenomena. To be consistent with the object of study that Smith assigned to science in the *History of Astronomy*, we must then see in those two works an attempt to explain the events that occur, in the social sphere, despite our intentions and/or alongside them. Which is equivalent to saying that science, whatever the territory in which it undertakes its investigations, has as its object the study of those unexpected phenomena which are not directly attributable to human action.[77]

This idea pervades all of Smith's research. It is already present when, in *Moral Sentiments*, it is explained that we are not born with a pre-formed self.

> Were it possible that a human creature could grow up to manhood in some solitary place, without any communication with his own species, he could no more think of his own character, of the propriety or demerit of his own sentiments and conduct, of the beauty or deformity of his own mind, than of the beauty or deformity of his own face.[78]

He would not be able to "easily see" all these things, he would not be able to see them "naturally", because he would have "no mirror" which can present them to his view; "bring him into society, and he is immediately provided with the mirror which he wanted before".[79]

It follows that the transformation of the brain into a human mind occurs through relations with others. Using the "mirror" metaphor and bearing in mind Smith's passage, Popper said that, "long before we attain consciousness and knowledge of ourselves, we have, normally, become aware of other persons, usually our parents"; and added that "a consciousness of self begins to develop through the medium of other persons; just as we learn to see ourselves in a mirror, so the child becomes conscious of himself by seeing his reflection in the mirror of other people's consciousness of himself".[80] Thus, brain accumulates an infinite variety of data on an "unstructured background", from which "a structure suddenly arises"; "and this happens completely unconsciously".[81] The brain does not plan its own growth, nor can it be programmed externally.[82]

This means that our *humanization* is an unintended consequence of social relationships. It is so when we come into the world: because our relationship with others communicates to us, without there being any awareness on our part, the rules of conduct and the yardsticks with which to "measure" everything that happens around us. And it is so for our entire lives. The need to live together and cooperate always drives us to co-adapt our actions. To do this, we resort to "sympathy", through which we try to account for the "situation" that elicits the passions of others or, more simply, the attitude of others towards us.[83] In other words, we try to see ourselves as others see us. It is an "imaginary change of place".[84] This is why Albert Salomon rightly wrote that Smithian *sympathy* cannot be made to coincide with "compassion, empathy or any imitation of feelings".[85] It is only an attempt to put ourselves in the place of our interlocutors, in order to observe and judge our behaviour through their expectations. It is a continuous "movement", from which we cannot escape: because respect for the expectations of others is what allows us to achieve our goals.

Therefore,

> every faculty in one man is the measure by which he judges of the like faculty in another. I judge of your sight by my sight, of your ear by my ear, of your reason by my reason, of your resentment by my resentment, of your love by my love. I neither have, nor can have, any other way of judging about them.[86]

"*It is thus that the general rules of morality are formed.*"[87] And these make us "*impartial spectators* of our own character and conduct".[88] The intersubjective relationship creates a sort of "third person", a two-faced Janus that incorporates the "perspective" of Ego and that of Alter.[89]

As Hume had already said, "the rules of morality [...] are not the conclusions of our reason".[90] They are a product of social interaction and the consequent co-adaptation of individual plans. Behind them is no intervention of the "invisible hand of Jupiter" or of a various imaginary population, which towers above us and dictates the rules of our lives. There is no direct will of individuals; and there is no will of a great planner. Of course, "man is generally considered by statesmen and projectors as the materials of a sort of political mechanism".[91] But "every individual [...] can, in his local situation, judge much better than any statesman or lawgiver can do for him";[92] and he

> who should attempt to direct private people in what manner they ought to employ their capitals, would not only load himself with a most unnecessary attention, but assume an authority which could safely be trusted, not only to no single person, but to no council or senate whatever, and which would nowhere be so dangerous as in the hands of a man who had folly and presumption enough to fancy himself fit to exercise it.[93]

The "unexpected events" that occur in the social field are therefore the result of interaction, of a process in which we participate and whose complexity escapes the control of any of us. We act intentionally to achieve our goals. And yet, to be able to implement our plans in whole or in part, each of us must try to adapt them to those of others. Social norms are the unplannable result of the marking out of the boundaries between the actions of each. In other words, we act intentionally to achieve our goals and, in doing so, we unintentionally fuel the birth of the conditions that make social cooperation possible.

This is why Smith, when he used the expression "invisible hand" in his *Moral Sentiments*, stripped it of that paternity "of Jupiter" that in the *History of Astronomy* accompanies "pusillanimous superstition"; and, dwelling on the dynamics of social cooperation, drew our attention to the intentional and unintentional outcomes of our actions. Consequently, he wrote: "though the sole end which they [the rich] propose from the labours of all the thousands whom they employ be the gratification of their own vain and insatiable desires, they divide with the poor the produce of all their improvements".[94] And he concluded that they are in this case guided by an "invisible hand";[95] that is to say, the eminently social character of human life means that no one can achieve their goals without interacting and cooperating with others. The pursuit of our purposes is intentional. However, we must provide services in order to obtain the cooperation of others, and in this way we unintentionally make it possible to achieve the aims of those who help us to achieve ours.

4.4   SMITH: DIVISION OF LABOUR AND "RULE OF LAW"

All this makes us understand the reasons why Smith opened the *Wealth of Nations* with a discussion of the division of labour, which he spoke about from a technical point of view. But what matters most here is what he wrote about the social division of labour.[96] He first acknowledged that "what is the work of one man, in a rude state of society, being that of several in an improved one": in "every improved society", the work "which is necessary to produce any one complete manufacture, is almost always divided among a great number of hands".[97] It follows that, with his own work, man can only obtain "a very small part" of the goods he needs; "He supplies the far greater part of them" through the work of others.[98] "He stands at all times in need of the cooperation and assistance of great multitudes, while his whole life is scarce sufficient to gain the friendship of a few persons".[99] Without the division of labour, "every man must have procured to himself every necessary convenience of life which he wanted", "all must have had the same duties to perform, and the same work to do" and "the most dissimilar geniuses" are not "of use to one another".[100]

However, the division of labour was not the product of the conscious planning of particularly acute minds. It was not the effect "of any human wisdom, which foresees and intends that general opulence to which it gives occasion";[101] it was the unintended consequence of man's attempt to better achieve their goals.[102] And it is what in turn leads us to contribute unintentionally to the pursuit of the ends of others. It is not without reason, turning to the metaphor that most characterized his work, that Smith wrote: "every individual", directing his activity "in such a way as its produce may be of the greatest value, he intends only his own gain, and he is in this, as in many other cases, led by an invisible hand to promote an end which was no part of his intention".[103]

Herein lies the explanation of what happens in the Great Society, in the situation, that is, in which everyone can exercise their freedom of choice and in which the division of labour and voluntary cooperation are fully realized. In this case, a unitary, compulsorily imposed hierarchy of ends is missing. Each actor has their own scale of preferences, which they do not have to account for to their counterparts, and which the counterparts, even if they were aware of them, might not agree with. Everyone pays with what they do best for what they do worst. The expression "invisible hand" is nothing more than a shorthand expression with which Smith laid particular emphasis on the fact that the pursuit of all our personal purposes necessarily entails the provision of services for the benefit of others.

Obviously, Smith did not neglect the normative *habitat* that makes unintended order possible. He wanted to write a work on the "general principles" of law and government. He had announced it on the last page of the first edition of *Moral Sentiments*.[104] When he issued the sixth edition of the same work, he declared that he had not completely "abandoned the design".[105] But the thread of his life snapped soon after. This does not deprive us of the elements we need to identify the theory of law that he would have liked to develop. On one page of *Moral Sentiments*, Smith wrote:

> Mere justice is, upon most occasions, but a negative virtue, and only hinders us from hurting our neighbour. The man who barely abstains from violating either the person or the estate, or the reputation, of his neighbours, has surely very little positive merit. He fulfils, however, all the rules of what is peculiarly called justice, and does every thing which his equals can with propriety force him to do, or which they can punish him for not doing. We may often fulfil all the rules of justice by sitting still and doing nothing.[106]

Consequently, to allow compatibility between actions, it is not necessary to prescribe their content. Individual freedom of choice has what is unjust as its only limit; and cooperation takes place on a voluntary basis. For the rest, co-adaptation occurs as a result of the free assessments of each; and this is exactly what the "rule of law" envisages.

It is a situation that is constantly threatened by that "insidious and crafty animal, vulgarly called a statesman or politician", who directs his judgements solely on the basis of the "momentary fluctuations of affairs".[107] He denies that each citizen, "pursuing his own interest", "promotes" that of others.[108] He does not recognize that "to hurt in any degree the interest of any one order of citizens, for no other purpose but to promote that of some other, is evidently contrary to that justice and equality of treatment which the sovereign owes to all the different orders of his subjects".[109] And not only that. On a deeper level, he attacks the gnoseological assumption on which the Great Society is based, because his interventionism is the clear manifestation of a refusal to accept the condition of ignorance and fallibility, to which we all are subject and which requires dispensing politics "from a duty, in the attempting to perform which" it is always "exposed to innumerable delusions, and for the proper performance of which no human wisdom or knowledge could ever be sufficient".[110]

One can thus understand why "in free countries, where the safety of government depends very much on the favourable judgment which the people may form of its conduct", it is "surely of the highest importance that they should not be disposed to judge rashly or capriciously concerning it".[111] It is necessary that the ruled not be fooled by the promises of the rulers. If this happens, the "rule of law" gives way to the "rule of men", to the illusion of an intentional order, from which everyone thinks they can benefit, but which always means an arbitrary kind of politics removed from any limitation and the forfeiting of the broader process of exploration of the unknown and correction of errors.[112]

In light of the above, it can be said that the theory of unintended consequences guided Smith's thought throughout his long career.[113] Not unlike Mandeville and Hume, Smith systematically showed how each of us, pursuing our own goals, unintentionally contributes to the realization of the goals of others. He travelled a very different path from that of Hutcheson.[114] Not surprisingly, commenting on Hutcheson's work, he wrote:

> Benevolence may, perhaps, be the sole principle of action in the Deity [...]. It is not easy to conceive what other motive an independent and all-perfect Being, who stands in need of nothing external, and whose happiness is complete in itself, can act from. But whatever may be the case with the Deity, so imperfect a creature as man, the support of whose existence requires so many things external to him, must often act from many, other motives.[115]

Even sharper is the well-known passage in the *Wealth of Nations*, in which Smith himself said: "It is not from the benevolence of the butcher, the brewer, or the baker, that we expect our dinner, but from their regard to their own interest."[116] *Self-love* cannot be erased.[117]

4.5　APPENDIX: ADAM FERGUSON

Adam Ferguson published the first edition of his best-known work, the *Essay on the History of Civil Society*, in 1767: after Smith's *Moral Sentiments*, but before the *Wealth of Nations*. Ferguson stressed, very effectively, the unintended origin of social institutions. It suffices to think of the following passage: "every step and every movement of the multitude, even in what are termed enlightened ages, are made with equal blindness to the future; and the nations stumble upon establishments, which are indeed the result of human action, but not the execution of any human design".[118]

The *Essay* was not judged positively by Hume and Smith. The latter believed that Ferguson had appropriated some of his ideas;[119] and Hume, although he had at first placed great hope in Ferguson's work, disapproved of some of the content. In a letter sent to Smith on 12 April 1759, he reported having read the *Treatise on Refinement*, which would later become the *Essay on the History of Civil Society*, and having found it much improved and liable, "with some amendments", to become an "admirable book", capable of showing "an elegant and singular genius".[120] And yet, when confronted with the definitive version of the work, Hume tried, addressing Hugh Blair and, through him, William Robertson, to discourage its publication: because its "failure", in addition to procuring "mortification" to the author, would have harmed the entire intellectual class, "at present in so flourishing a situation".[121]

As is well known, the appearance of the *Essay on the History of Civil Society* was an immediate success. Hume expressed his congratulations for this, but did not change his judgement. In a letter dated 19 March 1767 to Robertson, he wrote that he had asked Elizabeth Montagu for her evaluation of the work and that he had collected her reservations about the Scottish "style" of the work.[122]

What is at issue here? Since his theory of the social order does not concern itself with the motivations of the actor (it focuses on the fact that no one can achieve his goals without serving others), Hume could never have agreed with passages such as the following:

> It appears to be, in a particular manner, the object of sumptuary laws, and of the equal division of wealth, to prevent the gratification of vanity, to check the ostentation of superior fortune, and, by this means, to weaken the desire of riches, and to preserve in the breast of the citizen, that moderation and equity which ought to regulate his conduct [...]. Of all the nations whose history is known with certainty, the design itself, and the manner of executing it, appear to have been understood in Sparta alone.[123]

Ferguson was perfectly aware of his disagreement with Hume. In a letter sent to him on 17 April 1767, he wrote:

> I don't believe that there is in the whole list of created beings one that acts his part or fulfils better than man [...]. I write all this in hopes that when you see Mrs. Montagu you will mix some of my philosophy with your own. I am nevertheless somewhat angry with her for conjuring up the Spartan black broth against me [...]. I know that you are an admirer of the Athenians as well as Mrs. Montagu and, if I were to plead the cause of Sparta against her, I must appeal somewhere else.[124]

There is a fundamental ambivalence in Ferguson.[125] He used the theory of unintended consequences, but at the same time he was a supporter of the Spartan order. In a long letter to Smith on 23 June, George-Louis Le Sage wrote: "I have just finished reading the book of one of your compatriots, Mr Ferguson. It gave me great pleasure, but I was saddened to find praise of Sparta in it."[126]

NOTES

1. Mandeville formulated his "research programme" in the period prior to the publication of Montesquieu's earliest works. Hume formulated it later, but completed it earlier. For an extensive discussion of the relationships between Montesquieu and Hume, see Turco (2005, pp. 45–65) and the bibliography indicated therein.
2. Montesquieu ([1748] 1875–79d), p. 93.
3. Op. cit., p. 104.
4. Ibid.
5. Montesquieu ([1725] 1875–79b), p. 68. It is worth adding that, against Machiavellian politics, Montesquieu, in *Lettres persanes*, makes Usbek say: public law "is better understood in Europe than in Asia; and yet it must be said that the passions of princes, the suffering of the people, and the flattery of authors, have corrupted all its principles. At the present time, this law is a science which teaches princes to what length they may carry the violation of justice" (Montesquieu, [1721] 1875–79a, pp. 301–302). In the *Esprit des lois*, Montesquieu ([1748] 1875–79e, p. 460) also stated: "We begin to be cured of Machiavellianism and recover from it every day."
6. If norms and institutions are the product of social interaction, the inescapable consequence is their variability. Mandeville was aware of that. And Hume, after writing that "our situation with regard to both persons and things is in continuous fluctuation" (Hume, [1739–1740] 1930, vol. 2, p. 277), stated that "the principles upon which men reason in morals are always the same; though the conclusions which they draw are often very different" (Hume, [1751] 1902b, pp. 335–336); he added that we should not expect to find "the same laws in Berne, which prevail in London or Paris" (op. cit., p. 337); and he also pointed out that "the manners of a people change very considerably from one age to another, either by great alterations in their government, by the mixtures of new people or by the inconstancy to which all human affairs are subject" (Hume, 1742–1757] 1903, p. 211).

7. On Montesquieu's sources, see at greater length Dodds (1929).
8. Montesquieu ([1721] 1875–79a), p. 113.
9. Op. cit., p. 111.
10. Ibid.
11. Montesquieu ([1725] 1875–79b), p. 67. As is well known, this statement can be found on the first page of the first book of the *Esprit des lois* (Montesquieu, [1748] 1875–79d, p. 90).
12. Montesquieu ([1734] 1875–79c, p. 273). Montesquieu spoke of "moral and physical" causes. But he attributed greater weight to the former. No wonder, then, that he wrote: "The more the physical causes incline mankind to inaction, the more the moral causes should estrange them from it" (Montesquieu, [1748] 1875–79e, p. 155). For his part, Hume expressed himself more forcefully. He wrote that, even if its soil and climate remain unchanged, the "character of a nation" cannot remain "the same for a century together" (Hume, [1739–1740] 1930, vol. 2, p. 40). He went on to point out: "Athens and Thebes were but a short day's journey from each other, though the Athenians were as remarkable for ingenuity, politeness, and gaiety, as Thebans for dulness, rusticity, and a phlegmatic temper" (Hume, [1742–1757] 1903, p. 209). He added that it is not possible to attribute to air and climate the difference between the ways of life in Wapping and in St James (ibid.). And he noted that "the Chinese have the greatest uniformity of character imaginable, though the air and climate, in different parts of those vast dominions, admit of very considerable variations" (ibid.). In a letter sent on 10 April 1749, Hume drew Montesquieu's attention to some points in the *Esprit des lois*, but he did not mention the problem of "moral and physical" causes, to which he subsequently decided to devote (on 4 December 1754) a meeting of the *Select Society* of Edinburgh (Mossner, 2001, pp. 281–282).
13. Montesquieu ([1734] 1875–79c), p. 273.
14. Montesquieu ([1748] 1875–79d), p. 83.
15. Montesquieu ([1721] 1875–79a), pp. 215–216.
16. Op. cit., pp. 327–328. Usbek added: "Changes cannot be effected except by the prince or by the people: but there the princes take care to alter nothing, because possessed of such absolute power, they have all they can have: were they to make any change it could only be to their own injury. As to the subjects, should one of them form any design [...], it would be necessary to overturn at one blow a most formidable and unchanging power; for this he lacks time and means: but he has only to attack the source of that power, for which all he needs is an arm and a moment of time. The murderer mounts the throne, as the monarch leaves it and falls expiring at his feet" (op. cit., p. 328).
17. Montesquieu ([1734] 1875–79c), p. 222.
18. Montesquieu ([1748] 1875–79d), pp. 114–115.
19. Montesquieu ([1734] 1875–79c), p. 187.
20. Ibid. Montesquieu then added: "In a word, a government which is free, and thus always in turmoil, could not be preserved if it were not able to correct itself with its own laws."
21. Montesquieu ([1748] 1875–79d), p. 175.
22. Montesquieu ([1748] 1875–79e), p. 361.
23. Ibid. Pocock (1985, p. 122) renamed the concern expressed by Plato as "plainte de Rousseau". See more extensively Infantino (2020a), pp. 150–155.
24. Montesquieu ([1721] 1875–79a), p. 301.
25. Op. cit., pp. 81–82.

26. Op. cit., p. 336.
27. Montesquieu ([1725] 1875–79b), p. 67; ([1748] 1875–79d), p. 90.
28. Montesquieu ([1748] 1875–79d), p. 90.
29. Ibid.
30. Op. cit., p. 93. For his response to the accusation of atheism, see Montesquieu ([1748] 1875–79f), pp. 152–159.
31. Montesquieu ([1721] 1875–79a), p. 82.
32. Montesquieu ([1748] 1875–79d), p. 121.
33. Op. cit., pp. 123–124.
34. Op. cit., p. 131.
35. Op. cit., p. 135.
36. Op. cit., p. 133.
37. Op. cit., pp. 135–136.
38. Op. cit., p. 128.
39. Op. cit., pp. 88–89.
40. In the *Lettres persanes*, Montesquieu had already written: in England "you may see liberty flaming up again and again from discord and sedition; the prince, always tottering upon an immovable throne; a nation impatient, but prudent in its rage; and which, mistress of the sea [...], combines commerce with power" (Montesquieu, [1721] 1875–79a, p. 423).
41. Montesquieu ([1748] 1875–79d), p. 132.
42. Op. cit., p. 162.
43. Op. cit., p. 154.
44. Ibid.
45. Rawson (1969), pp. 227–229.
46. Rousseau ([1750] 1997), p. 11. The Spartan model was always Rousseau's point of reference. See more extensively Infantino (2019), pp. 41–42.
47. Suffice it to think of Diderot, d'Holbach and Mably. For a detailed discussion of the subject, see Rawson (1969) and Guerci (1979). For more concise references, see Infantino (2003, pp. 212–223) and Pellicani (2011, p. 185). This does not mean that all the Enlightenment thinkers suffered from "Laconomania". Voltaire ([1752] 1822, vol. 6, pp. 413) did not hesitate to affirm: "The luxury of Athens created great men in all branches of human activity: Sparta had only a few leaders of armies who were even lesser in number than in other cities." As with all cultural movements, the French Enlightenment and the *Encyclopédie* embraced a variety of positions. See, among others, Hubert (1923; 1928), Cassirer ([1932] 1967) and Israel (2009).
48. Jaucourt (1765), p. 152.
49. In the social order attributed to divine will, there is an invisible population that oversees the intentions of the subjects. Being unable to use the same instrument, totalitarianism resorts to permanent mobilization, which means that it subjects individuals to a continuous process of "alteration", which prevents them from thinking critically and distancing themselves from the existent. It is no coincidence that Rousseau ([1762] 1974, p. 49) aimed to give the "general will" a "strength beyond the power of any individual will"; and he expressed the wish that the "laws of the nations, like the laws of nature, could never be broken by any human power". Totalitarianism also makes use of systematic *self-criticism* and use of informers, which is a means whereby the confession of crimes which have never been committed can be extorted (Infantino, 2020a, pp. 99–100).

50. It would later be Spencer ([1877–1896] 1906, vol. 2, pp. 473–642) who emphasized the distinction between voluntary cooperation and coercive cooperation.
51. Montesquieu ([1748] 1875–79e), p. 264.
52. Montesquieu ([1748] 1875–79d), p. 176.
53. Plutarch ([A], 24, I.), where one also reads that everyone "always had a prescribed regimen and employment in public service, considering that they belonged entirely to their country and not to themselves".
54. Op. cit., 9, I.
55. This is how Pericles described it: "We throw open our city to the world, and never by alien acts exclude foreigners from any opportunity of learning or observing, although the eyes of an enemy may occasionally profit by our liberality" (Thucydides, [A], II, 39).
56. Montesquieu ([1748] 1875–79d), p. 124.
57. That is why Constant ([1819] 1872b, p. 551) rightly observed that Montesquieu attributed the "difference to the republic and the monarchy", while "it ought instead to be attributed to the opposed spirit of ancient and modern times. Citizens of republics, subjects to monarchy, all want pleasures, and indeed no-one, in the present conditions of societies can help wanting them. The people [the English people] most attached to their liberty in our days, before the emancipation of France, was also the most attached to all the pleasure of life; and it valued its liberty especially because it saw in this the guarantee of the pleasures which it cherished. In the past, where there was liberty, people could bear hardship. Now, wherever there is hardship, despotisms are necessary for people to resign themselves to it."
58. Montesquieu ([1748] 1875–79d), p. 158. For further clarification of Montesquieu's starting position, it is worth mentioning one of the few fragments of the *Traité des devoirs*: "If I could for a moment cease to think that I am a Christian, I could not do without placing the destruction of the sect of Zeno in the category of the misfortunes of the human race; it pushed to excess only the things in which there was greatness: the contempt of pleasures and pain"; Montesquieu ([1725] 1875–79b, p. 67) then added: "the stoics, born for society, all believed that their destiny was to do all they could for it [...], it seemed that only the happiness of others could increase theirs". One can thus understand his hostility towards Epicurus, whose doctrine he blamed for having contributed, "towards the close of the republic", to corrupt "the minds and genius of the people", as had happened before with the Greeks (Montesquieu, ([1734] 1875–79c, p. 195). On the impossibility of shedding light on the dynamics of the Great Society through the doctrines of the Stoics, see Bonar (1893, p. 50).
59. As is well known, Machiavelli ([1531] 1883, p. 42) instead argued: "we must take it as a rule to which there are very few if any exceptions, that no commonwealth or kingdom ever has salutary institutions given it from the first or has its institutions recast in an entirely new mould, unless by a single person [... Nay,] it must be from one man that it receives its institutions at first, and upon one man that all similar reconstruction must depend".
60. Montesquieu ([1748] 1875–79d), pp. 158–159. Following Pocock (1985, p. 194), Lenci (2005, p. 440) appropriately wrote that in this way what was realized was the affirmation of "commercial humanism" over "civic humanism", that is, over the "republican tradition that was based on the Machiavellian concept of virtue and had been embodied by characters such as James Harrington, Algernon Sidney" and others. On this tradition, see Fink (1962).

61. Montesquieu ([1748] 1875–79e), p. 8.
62. Hayek (1978), pp. 138–139.
63. Rawson (1969), p. 350.
64. Smith ([1762–1764] 1976–83d), p. 231.
65. Ibid.
66. Smith ([1795] 1976–83c), p. 103. Obviously, Smith was referring to the predictions made by Edmund Halley.
67. As is well known, the *History of Astronomy* is one of the essays published posthumously by testamentary executors, Joseph Black and James Hutton. With regard to these essays, Schumpeter (1954, vol. 1, p. 221) wrote: "I dare say that those who do not know these essays cannot have an adequate idea of Smith's intellectual stature. I would go as far as to say that, if the fact were not undeniable, no one would attribute to the author of the *Wealth of Nations* the ability to write them." Schumpeter also judged the essay on the *History of Astronomy*, which is the greatest of the posthumously published works a real "pearl" (ibid.).
68. Smith ([1795] 1976–83c), p. 49.
69. Ibid.
70. Ibid.
71. Op. cit., p. 50.
72. Ibid.
73. Ibid.
74. Op. cit., pp. 112–113, emphasis added.
75. This is the same question raised by Hume; see Chapter 3, note 66. Several passages from the *History of Astronomy* show Hume's influence on Smith. The friendship between the two can be traced back to the autumn of 1749. Hume had then returned from his diplomatic mission to Vienna and Turin; and Smith had already been delivering lectures from the previous year for the Edinburgh Philosophical Society, of which Hume was one of the principal exponents (cf. Rasmussen, 2017, pp. 45–46). The first draft of the *Dialogues Concerning Natural Religion*, which appeared posthumously, is from the summer of 1749, while the *Natural History of Religion* was published in 1757. It is easy to believe that the subject was a topic in their long conversations in those years.
76. Smith ([1740–1790] 1976–83e), p. 168.
77. Popper (1991), pp. 342–343.
78. Smith ([1759] 1976–83a), p. 110.
79. Ibid. The "mirror" idea had already been used by Hume (see the text at note 93 in Chapter 3).
80. Popper (1977, vol. 1, pp. 109–110), who (op. cit., p. 111, note 7) then quoted Smith's passage.
81. The statement is by Lorenz, taken from Popper and Lorenz (1985), pp. 26–27.
82. See Hayek (1988, p. 22), who said: "What we call mind is not something that the individual is born with, as he is born with his brain, or something that the brain produces, but something that his genetic equipment (e.g. a brain of a certain size and structure) helps him to acquire, as he grows up, from his family and adult fellows by absorbing the results of a tradition that is not genetically transmitted."
83. Smith ([1759] 1976–83a), p. 12. Smith took the concept of *sympathy* from Hume ([1739–1740] 1930, vol. 2, pp. 82–83). For a more detailed discussion, see Morrow (1923).
84. Stewart ([1793] 1980), p. 281.
85. Salomon (1945), pp. 28–29.

86. Smith ([1759] 1976–83a), p. 19.
87. Op. cit., p. 159, emphasis added.
88. Op. cit., p. 114, emphasis added.
89. Op. cit., pp. 135 and 191. It is perhaps not accidental that Ortega y Gasset ([1928] 1946–83h), writing many years after Smith, spoke of the social element as a "third character", born from interaction. One can trace the influence of Simmel (1908, pp. 85–86) on Ortega's work. Simmel (1910, pp. 102–112) also spoke of the social as a "third kingdom". Popper (1979, p. 106) himself used the expression "third world" for a shared (that is, social) world.
90. See note 48 in Chapter 3.
91. Stewart ([1793] 1980), p. 322. See also Scott (1937), pp. 117–120.
92. Smith ([1776] 1976–83b), vol. 1, p. 456.
93. Ibid. Smith (op. cit., p. 531) further stressed: "the law ought always to trust people with the care of their own interest, as in their local situations they must generally be able to judge better than it than the legislator can do". Here there is the problem of the dispersion of knowledge of time and place. As is well known, this problem was taken up during the twentieth century by Hayek (1949, pp. 77–91).

It should also be remembered that Smith ([1759] 1976–83a, pp. 233–234) wrote in *Moral Sentiments*: "The man of system [...] is apt to be very wise in his own concept; and is often so enamoured with the supposed beauty of his own ideal plan of government, that he cannot suffer the smallest deviation from any part of it [...]. He seems to imagine that he can arrange the different members of a great society, with as much case as the hand arranges the different pieces upon a chess-board; he does not consider that the pieces upon the chess-board have no other principle of motion besides that which the hand impresses upon them; but that, in the great chess-board of human society, every single piece has a principle of motion of its own, altogether different from that which the legislature might choose to impress upon it."

As can be seen from Smith's notice (op. cit., p. 3), this passage was introduced in the sixth edition (1790) of *Moral Sentiments*. See also Morrow (1923), p. 76.
94. Smith ([1759] 1976–83a), p. 184.
95. Ibid.
96. Smith ([1776] 1976–83b), vol. 1, pp. 13–14, note 1) acknowledged his debt to Mandeville, from whom he also took examples.
97. Op. cit., pp. 135 and 15–16.
98. Op. cit., p. 37.
99. Op. cit., p. 26.
100. Op. cit., pp. 29–30.
101. Op. cit., p. 25.
102. It is well known that Durkheim ([1893] 1964, p. 238) stated that there is a "classic" explanation in "political economy", that "appears so simple and so evident", "unconsciously admitted by a host of thinkers", according to which the division of labour is a direct consequence of the pursuit of happiness. Durkheim's mistake was not understanding that the evolutionary tradition Smith belongs to cannot be assimilated to the rationalist tradition of Bentham and his followers. Durkheim had a poor grasp of political economy and its history. See more extensively Infantino (1998, p. 86).
103. Smith ([1776] 1976–83b), vol. 1, p. 456.
104. Smith ([1759] 1976–83a), p. 342.

105. Op. cit., p. 3.
106. Op. cit., p. 82. Smith then added: "The wisdom of every state or commonwealth endeavours, as well as it can, to employ the force of the society to restrain those who are subject to its authority from hurting or disturbing the happiness of one another" (ibid., p. 218). Smith's pupil Millar, for his part, stated: "Justice requires no more than that I should abstain from hurting my neighbour, in his person, his property, or his reputation; that I should pay my debts, or perform the service, which by my contracts, or by the course of my behaviour, I have given him reason to expect from me [...], the line of duty suggested by this *mere negative virtue*, can be clearly marked, and its boundaries distinctly ascertained" (Millar, 1803, vol. 4, p. 267, emphasis added).
107. Smith ([1776] 1976–83b), vol. 1, p. 468.
108. Op. cit., p. 456.
109. Op. cit., vol. 2, p. 654.
110. Op. cit., p. 687.
111. Op. cit., p. 788. See, at greater length, Haakonssen (1981), pp. 89–93.
112. It thus occurs that "every system which endeavours, either, by extraordinary encouragements, to draw towards a particular species of industry a greater share of the capital of the society than what would naturally go to it; or, by extraordinary restraints, to force from a particular species of industry some share of the capital which would otherwise be employed in it; is in reality subversive of the great purpose which it means to promote" (Smith, [1776] 1976–83b, vol. 2, p. 687). These interventions delay, rather than accelerate, "the progress of the society towards real wealth and greatness"; and decrease "the real value of the annual produce" (ibid.). The result is therefore exactly the opposite of the one that we claim to be pursuing.
113. Smith (op. cit., vol. 1, pp. 386–418) also explained with the same theory the birth of market society. His explanation was then accepted by Ferguson (1792, vol. 1, p. 314) and by Millar (1803, vol. 2, p. 81). On Smith's extensive use of the scheme of unintended consequences in explaining social phenomena, see Infantino (2020b) and the bibliography indicated therein.
114. See Cannan (1904, p. xlvi); Schumpeter (1914, p. 52); and Hayek (1978, p. 252).
115. Smith ([1759] 1976–83a), p. 305.
116. Smith ([1776] 1976–83b), vol. 1, pp. 26–27.
117. Hutcheson always believed the opposite (Smith, [1759] 1976–83a, p. 303). What is quoted in the text shows that between what is claimed in *Moral Sentiments* and what is stated in the *Wealth of Nations* perfectly coincide. However, it is well known that, in the German context, initially the *Umschwungstheorie* was formulated; this claimed that the "moral sentiments" philosopher had to be considered different from the economist who based action on personal interest. This thesis was also espoused by scholars such as Viner (1927, p. 201) and Sen (1987, p. 28). Raphael and Macfie (1976, p. 20) strenuously argued that the so-called "Adam Smith-Problem" is a "pseudo-problem, based on ignorance and misunderstanding". For a more extensive discussion, see Infantino (2020b), pp. 228–230.
118. Ferguson ([1767] 1966), p. 122.
119. Smith thought that Ferguson had taken advantage of the notes transcribed by students at the lectures he gave in Glasgow between 1748 and 1751. In particular, he believed that the author of the *Essay* had appropriated the considerations he had made on the subject of the division of labour. However, Ferguson shifted his

focus onto another topic. He claimed to be indebted to Montesquieu, thus wanting to link himself to the theory of the stages of development that Montesquieu formulated and from which both had drawn inspiration. In opposition to Ferguson's claims, Oncken (1909, pp. 129–137) endorsed Smith's position, replacing the problem of the division of labour back at the centre of the dispute. Similarly, see Kettler (1965, pp. 74–75), Hamowy (1968, pp. 249–259) and the bibliography cited therein. On Montesquieu and the influence of his theory of the stages of development on the Scottish Enlightenment, cf. Sebastiani (2005, pp. 213–226).
120. Greig (1932), vol. 1, p. 304.
121. Op. cit., vol. 2, p. 12.
122. Op. cit., pp. 131–132. See also the subsequent letter (1 April 1767) to Hugh Blair (ibid., pp. 133–134).
123. Ferguson ([1767] 1966), p. 158.
124. Ferguson (1767), pp. 2–3. Obviously, Ferguson could not have asked Hume for support in defending the cause of Sparta. Suffice it to see what Hume wrote about the Spartans in his essay *Of Commerce* (Hume, [1742–1757] 1903, pp. 263–269).
125. Kettler (1965), p. 223.
126. Smith ([1740–1790] 1976–83e), p. 128. Hume believed that Ferguson's book could not enjoy lasting success (Greig, 1932, vol. 2, p. 383). According to Schumpeter (1954, p. 184, note 16), the *Essay* enjoyed "undeserved fame". Meek (1976, p. 150) on the other hand wrote that "undoubtedly" it is "one of the most notable works of the epoch".

5. Initial continuities and discontinuities

> Government is [...] no longer regarded as the head of society, destined to unite in a bundle and to direct towards a *common end* all individual activities [...] where a general and organised action is not exercised, there is no *society*. (Auguste Comte)
> As [...] there is no social sensorium, the welfare of the aggregate, considered apart from that of the units, is not an end to be sought. The society exists for the benefit of its members; not members for the benefit of society. (Herbert Spencer)

5.1 IMMEDIATE SCOTTISH INFLUENCES IN POLITICAL THEORY: EDMUND BURKE AND BENJAMIN CONSTANT

Edmund Burke and Benjamin Constant are among those who most promptly adopted the "Scottish" conception of the social sciences. The former was undoubtedly advantaged by the fact that he interacted directly with Hume and Smith. The latter, at a time when Smith was still alive and the "Athens of the North" continued to shed light on social phenomena, benefited from spending an intense (albeit brief) period of study there.

In 1756, Burke published *A Philosophical Inquiry into the Origin of Our Ideas of the Sublime and the Beautiful*, where he stated, among other things: "sympathy must be considered as a sort of *substitution* by which we are put into the place of another man and affected in as many respects as he is affected".[1] Which is equivalent to saying that Burke realized that social norms are the product of a process of co-adaptation of actions. Hume's influence on Burke's work is clear; and Smith, at that time engaged in drafting *Moral Sentiments*, was able to grasp the converging strands between his research programme and the work produced by Burke, who in turn realized, the value of Smith's first great work, when he received a copy from Hume, and reviewed it favourably in the *Annual Register*.[2] Thus was born an extraordinary intellectual bond. As Dugald Stewart referred, Smith believed at the time that, if Burke had decided to accept "a chair", this would have been "a great acquisition" for the University of Glasgow.[3] Subsequently, Smith himself was quick to see in Burke "the only man" who in the economic field, even without any prior agreement, expressed thoughts coincident with his own.[4] The two men frequented with each other mainly in the period, following the publication of the *Wealth of Nations*, spent by Smith in London.[5]

Therefore, it is not surprising to find in Burke's thought the gnoseological postulates which were a fixture in guiding Smith's investigations. This is clearly borne out in the following statement: "I cannot conceive how any man can have brought himself to that pitch of presumption, to consider his country as nothing but *carte blanche* upon which he may scribble whatever he pleases".[6] As we know, the expression a man driven to "that pitch of presumption" is taken almost literally from the *Wealth of Nations*.[7] It suggests that, to deal with problems, we need the "aid of more minds".[8] "Self-sufficiency and arrogance" are inexorable companions of those who "have never experienced a wisdom greater than their own".[9] And it is not enough to add in a

> commission all the directors of the two academies to the directors of the *Caisse d'Escompte*, one old experienced peasant is worth them all. I have got more information, upon a curious and interesting branch of husbandry, in a short conversation with a Carthusian monk, than I have derived from all the Bank directors that I have ever conversed with.[10]

Consequently, the social process must be broadened as much as possible; and we must always have a "strong impression of the *ignorance and fallibility of mankind*".[11]

It follows that social norms and institutions *incorporate* much more than the limited and fallible knowledge of individual actors; and it is to be appreciated that "many of our thinkers" use their skills to discover the "latent wisdom" contained in social rules.[12] These are produced by the social process, as unintended results of actions individually directed to other purposes; and they are in turn the conditions that make social cooperation possible. In other words, no one can achieve their goals without doing something for the benefit of another. By mutually submitting to social rules, everyone obtains the cooperation of others and contributes, albeit unintentionally, to the achievement of the other's goals.[13] In social norms and institutions, there is therefore a "latent wisdom", because they contain a response, although one which is never definitive, to the problem of the co-adaptation of actions.[14]

It is a continuous exploration: "the liberties and the restrictions vary with times and circumstances [...], they cannot be settled" once and for all.[15] And it is a path in which we cannot avoid mistakes: "that which in the first instance is prejudicial may be excellent in its remoter operation" and "very plausible schemes, with very pleasing commencements, have often shameful and lamentable conclusions".[16] Since omniscience is an attribute of no person, we must avoid "absolute monarchy"; and we must also avoid "absolute democracy".[17] Burke called upon Aristotle in his support;[18] and it is known that the Stagirite had warned against the type of democracy that is "comparable to the tyrannical form of monarchy".[19] The analogy lies in the fact that "both exercise despotic control over the better classes, and the decrees voted by the assembly are like the commands issued in a tyranny, and the demagogues and the flatterers are the same people or a corresponding class, and either set has the very strongest influence with the respective ruling power".[20] In such situations, laws are not "sovereign"; and, where this occurs, there is no "constitution".[21] There is also no democracy "in the proper sense", because no decree is "universal".[22]

The "rule of men" does not make our freedom of choice possible and aggravates the consequences produced by our condition of ignorance and fallibility. This means that the discussions "which lacerate the commonwealth" should not have as their object the search for individuals to whom to entrust the exercise of power; they should concern "the manner in which it is to be exercised".[23] This inevitably leads to the relinquishment of any privileged source of knowledge and the affirmation of the "rule of law", intended as a regulatory *habitat* in which to house the process of exploring the unknown and correcting errors.

Although it has been written that Smith and Burke can be considered "complementary", the former's influence on the latter weighed more heavily.[24] And his influence also appears to have been very strong on Benjamin Constant, who gave us a direct testimony of the intellectual fervour to be found in the Scottish capital. He wrote:

> engaging in studies was fashionable among the young in Edinburgh, who joined various literary and philosophical associations. I also became a member of some and, albeit English was not my tongue, I distinguished myself as a writer and a speaker. I established very close relationships with a number of people, many of whom, in their maturity, attained a certain fame. These included Mackintosh, currently Royal Minister of Justice in Bombay, [and] Laing, one of the best continuers of Robertson's.[25]

Theodora Zemek rightly wrote that in Edinburgh Constant acquired "a body of presuppositions, a way of thinking, a historical method and a 'scientific' approach to moral philosophy".[26] This is so true that, "if the moral and historical theory of the Scottish Enlightenment is not taken into account, if the fact that Constant was in Edinburgh while Smith, Ferguson and Dugald Stewart were in residence is ignored, then it becomes impossible to grasp the spirit which pervades and unifies Benjamin Constant's thought".[27] Indeed, "viewed outside the context of the Scottish Enlightenment", it may appear "schismatic and confusing".[28]

Constant took the "Scottish" path. And he wrote:

> The imagination can invent a singularly useful application of unlimited social authority, supposing it to always be exercised in favour of reason, the interest of all and justice, capable of unfailingly choosing means with a noble nature and certain

success, and being able to subjugate the faculties of man without degrading them – capable, in a word, of acting in the same way the devout conceive of the action of providence, combining together, that is, the force of command and the conviction which reaches the depths of people's hearts.[29]

But can we conceive of power in the same way as providence and, for that reason, make it unlimited? Constant replied: to do this, it is necessary to consider the

> government, if not infallible, as more enlightened than the ruled. For in order to intervene in the relations between individuals with greater wisdom than they themselves could employ or to guide the development of their faculties or the use of their means with greater success than would be achievable by their own judgement, one would need to possess the certain prerogative of distinguishing better than they between what is advantageous and what is harmful.[30]

We also need to suppose that, "if government, despite its greater enlightenment, makes mistakes, these will be less disastrous than those made by individuals".[31]

It is therefore not possible to look at rulers as a privileged source of knowledge or a "superior wisdom".[32] They are subjected to the same condition of ignorance and fallibility that we all share. Those to whom we confer power "are subject, like all others, to error";[33] and "use their own errors as pretexts" to justify other decisions from which there descend further errors.[34] Thus, every "extension of the invested authority in invested rulers" contributes to creating a "blind force".[35] Mistakes are nothing more than unintended consequences of a negative nature.

What can be done? It is necessary to limit the sphere of intervention of the public authority, so that there be competing decisions.[36] There is a need for a regulatory *habitat* that allows everyone to exercise their freedom of choice and thereby mobilize their knowledge and resources. This is the condition that makes it possible to institutionalize a process of *trial and error*.

However, we remain with the problem of how to prevent the individual actor from infringing the scope of the autonomy of another. The "rightly understood" interest of every human being is to benefit from the cooperation of others.[37] This must be done in compliance with the "rules of justice".[38] These are not rules that dictate an obligatory hierarchy of ends. They merely prevent the actors from "harming each other".[39] They do not impose us "to do good"; they only prevent us from "doing evil".[40] They give rise to an "abstract order", which leaves undetermined the order which will concretely come about (as a result of the actions undertaken by each person within their own freedom of choice). Each intentionally exchanges means with others. But the order is not the product of anyone's plans. We are within the scope of the *utility of rules* or the "rule of law".[41]

Although Constant was critical of some of Burke's judgements, they both benefited from Smith's influence. It was Burke who foresaw that revolutionary extremism would lead the head of the army to become the "master" of France;[42] and it was Constant who reflected on the consequences of the Terror.[43]

5.2 INSIDE ECONOMIC THEORY: UTILITARIAN IN THE BROAD SENSE AND UTILITARIAN IN THE NARROW SENSE

What the "Darwinians before Darwin" argued shows that the expression "classical economists" encompasses two research traditions which must be clearly distinguished. The evolutionists can be considered utilitarian in a broad sense. They understood that the transformation of the brain into a human mind was not the product of conscious planning; there was therefore no first man and there was no *beginning* of society. They were aware that each person's knowledge is partial and fallible and that, to take advantage of the positive unintended outcomes of human actions and to defend against the negative ones, it is necessary to institutionalize an extensive process of exploration of the unknown and correction of errors. They recognized the condition of scarcity, which gave rise to the economic dimension of life.[44] They relinquished the pretension to impose a configuration dictated by some authority (divine and/or human) on social reality. They revealed that there is a need for general and abstract rules that permit the broadest development of the process of social cooperation: because this favours the birth of the "unforeseeable" and the "unpredictable", those things, that is, that individuals are not able to plan and that they will want only when the process of cooperation itself makes them available.[45]

As we already know (cf. Chapter 3, Section 3.5), alongside utilitarianism in the broad sense, there also, however, exists utilitarianism in the strict sense, which is the "psychologistic version of the social contract".[46] This operates "with the idea of a *beginning of society*, and with the idea of a human nature and a human psychology as they existed prior to society".[47] The social actors "have no properties but those which are derived from, or may resolved into, the laws of the nature of individual man".[48] Therefore, it is no surprise that Jeremy Bentham wrote:

> Among principles adverse to that of utility, that which at this day seems to have most influence in matters of government, is what may be called the principle of sympathy and antipathy. By the principle of sympathy, I mean that principle which approves or disapproves of certain actions, not on account of their tending to

augment the happiness, nor yet on account of their tending to diminish the happiness of the party whose interest is in question, but merely because a man finds himself disposed to approve or disapprove of them.[49]

Thus, utilitarianism in the strict sense precludes the possibility of understanding that *sympathy* is not a sentimental concept. It is the instrument by means of which we put ourselves in the position of the other, to try to see how he judges our actions, to try to identify, that is, the expectations that we must take into account in order to obtain the cooperation of others: because it is not only what we intend to pursue which is important; equally important is what we know (and are willing to do) for others, without whose intervention all our projects remain unfulfilled and unworkable.

If we adopt Bentham's approach, we remain blind to the process of social interaction and the mutual co-adaptation of actions. And we would have to follow John Stuart Mill who, consistently with what Bentham said, stated: "political economy concerns mankind as occupied solely" to satisfy the "desire" of "accumulating wealth, and employing that wealth in the production of other wealth".[50] This is the idea of *homo oeconomicus*, the inadequacy of which cannot be in any way concealed. This is in particular shown by the fact that, if the economic dimension of human action coincided with the simple "desire" of "accumulating wealth", it would be sufficient to suppress this desire in order to make the economic aspect of life disappear. This does not occur: because even individuals who are capable of containing the extent of their desire for enrichment must always come to terms with the condition of scarcity; and this is not avoided even by those who live in social formations where this desire is subjected to severe control or it is even attempted to suppress it completely.

If we follow the path indicated by the utilitarian tradition in the strict sense, we must go on to attribute economic characteristics only to actions aimed at the hoarding of wealth, whereas the economic dimension, precisely because we can never free ourselves from scarcity, is present in every human action. The fact is that what are erroneously called economic actions constitute only that portion relating to the search for and the use of (scarce) means in the pursuit of purposes that are not of an economic character.

Utilitarianism proper is therefore located in a territory which is quite separate from that of evolutionism. It did not anticipate Darwin; and, after the appearance of the *Origin of Species*, it was incapable of absorbing the Darwinian lesson. This is shown in particular by the career of John Stuart Mill. In this regard, Bertrand Russell appropriately wrote:

> It is rather surprising that Mill was so little influenced by Darwin and the theory of evolution. This is the more curious as he frequently quotes Herbert Spencer. He

seems to have accepted the Darwinian theory but without realizing its implications. In the chapter "on Classification" of his *Logic*, he speaks of "natural kinds" in an entirely pre-Darwinian fashion, and even suggests that the recognized species of animals and plants are *infimae species* in the scholastic sense, although Darwin's book on the *Origin of Species* proved this view to be untenable. It was natural that the first edition of his *Logic*, which appeared in 1843, should take no account of the theory of evolution, but it is odd that no modifications were made in later editions.[51]

Russell added: "I do not think that he [Mill] ever imaginatively conceived of man as one among animals or escaped from the Eighteenth-century belief that man is fundamentally rational."[52]

As Russell's statements show, there is in Mill (and in utilitarianism in the strict sense) an inability to recognize that nature and all human life are driven by an evolutionary process of an ateleological character. From an economic standpoint, Mill foreshadowed the "stationary state";[53] and, from the social standpoint, he believed that the future could be intentionally determined, through those "artificial means" that form "the noblest and most beneficial portions of the political art".[54] In this way, the "rule of law" gives way to the "rule of men". Politics is the independent variable of the social system. This is why Halévy rightly argued that, in Bentham and his followers, "the legislator is the great dispenser" of everything.[55] There is no limitation of power at all. The order is consciously decided.[56]

Consequently, we cannot speak of "classical economics" as a homogeneous and close-knit tradition of research. Joseph A. Schumpeter pointed this out.[57] He arrived at this conclusion by focusing on the political positions of the various authors involved. And yet, even more than political, the differences are methodological, they relate to, that is, the different gnoseological assumptions on which evolutionists and utilitarians in the strict sense based their research. These are problems that, even after Darwin, reared their heads again within "neo-classical economics". Carl Menger was an evolutionist. But William S. Jevons and Léon Walras were strictly utilitarians. Jevons was directly inspired by Bentham. Significantly, he declared that "pleasure and pain are undoubtedly the ultimate objects of the calculus of Economics";[58] and he assigned to economic theory the study of the ways in which to satisfy "our wants to the utmost with the least effort".[59] Walras thought of social science as a "mechanics of moral forces".[60] He believed he could "scientifically" establish a "law of human activity", in the same way as "the law of the earth's movement around the sun".[61] Therefore, in the work of Jevons and Walras, there is a clear "constructivist" ambition, which prevents us from escaping from the narrow horizon of intentional order.[62] This contradicts the discovery of the subjective basis of value.

Menger positioned himself on the opposite side. The anthropological traits of *homo mengerianus* are ignorance and fallibility. He is not a "lightning calculator";[63] he is "ill-informed, plagued with uncertainty, forever hovering between alluring hopes and haunting fears, and congenitally incapable of making finely calibrated decisions".[64] His actions are always accompanied by unintended consequences, to which we owe the unplanned birth of so many social institutions. Language, the family, the city, the State, the law, money, customs were born "without legislative compulsion, even without any consideration of public interest, simply through the impulse of *individual* interest and as a result of the activation of these interests".[65]

Individual actions and unintended consequences go hand in hand. The man who acts cannot control or predict the entire sequence of the results produced by his actions. There is a social process of which we cannot foresee all the consequences.

Menger was aware of the fracture between the approach of evolutionism and that of utilitarianism in the strict sense. This is borne out by the fact that, after a brief exchange of letters, he formulated the following judgement to Walras by way of conclusion: "A conformity does not exist between us. There is an analogy of concepts in a few points but not in the decisive questions."[66] Hayek did well to argue that Menger "was among the first in modern times consciously to revive the methodological individualism of Adam Smith".[67] But the founder of the Austrian School would not have agreed. Let's see why.

From the preface to this volume, we know that "methodological individualism" coincides with what Menger called the "compositive method" and that, in the study of social phenomena, it requires starting from the simplest elements and then working towards complexity.[68] If this is considered, it does not seem that Hayek's statement can be disputed. But Menger, in a page of his *Untersuchungen*, wrote that "Adam Smith and his school" aspired to the "*pragmatic* [intentional] understanding of economy", so they were precluded from the theoretical understanding of the "broad realm of unintentionally created social structures".[69] And that was not all. A few lines later, Menger added that Edmund Burke was the "first" to show, "with full awareness", that "numerous institutions of his country, which were to a high degree of common benefit and filled every Briton with pride, were not the result of positive legislation or of conscious common will of society directed towards establishing this, but the unintended result of historical development".[70]

What can be said about such judgements? Menger placed Smith in a theoretical area which was exactly opposite to the one he actually occupied, thus neglecting his overall theoretical design and the influence he (and Hume) exerted on Burke's work. It is therefore true that it was the latter's ideas, just as argued by the Austrian scholar, that provided Friedrich von Savigny with the arguments he used to affirm that, "at least originally" and "like language", law "is not the product [...] of an activity of public authorities aimed at producing it".[71] But Burke, who was always hostile to the myth of the Great Legislator and who was firmly attached to the social process, provided what constitutes the greatest acquisition of the "Scottish philosophers of the eighteenth century".[72]

Since he avoided identifying Burke's intellectual debts, Menger (if he had been alive) would not have accepted the link Hayek attributed to him. In support of his criticism of Smith, he would have reiterated that in the *Wealth of Nations* there is a reference to the labour theory of value, a version of the theory that presents the economic value of goods as determined by the cost of production;[73] which is what was done by his most immediate followers (Eugen von Boehm-Bawerk and Friedrich von Wieser).[74] But here, following the lesson on method taught by Weber, we need to assess whether the importance attributed to Smith's work should depend on his contribution to the birth of the social sciences (and the explanation of the unintended order) or on the reference, which is equivalent to an exclusive *petitio principii*, to the labour theory of value. And it should also be remembered that, in the logic of Mandeville, Hume and Smith, social values, including economic ones, are produced by the intersubjective relationship. It is no coincidence that Mandeville wrote that everything that is human originated as a consequence "of the reciprocal services, which men do to each other".[75] Hume stated that precious metal "is not riches, as it is [...] endowed with certain qualities of solidity, weight, and fusibility; but only as it has a relation to the pleasures and conveniences of life".[76] Smith pointed out that "every faculty in one man is the measure by which he judges of the like faculty in another";[77] and he took pains to point out that "consumption is the sole end and purpose of all production".[78]

Recognizing that, Menger might, even before Hayek, have shed light on the fracture that separates the "Darwinians before Darwin" from the exponents of utilitarianism in the strict sense; and he might have more adequately highlighted the points where his theoretical system converged with and diverged from that of Jevons and Walras.[79]

5.3 INSIDE SOCIOLOGY: THE DISCONTINUITY OF AUGUSTE COMTE AND THE CONTINUITY OF HERBERT SPENCER

As is well known, it was Auguste Comte who coined the term "sociology". And he made it "equivalent" to the expression "social physics", which he himself had introduced. In this way, he was confident of "being able to designate with a single name that complementary part of natural philosophy that refers to the positive study of the set of fundamental laws proper to social phenomena".[80]

Comte was hostile to the idea of unintended order. This is already clear in the *Prospectus des travaux nécessaires pour réorganiser la société*, which later became his *Plan de travaux*. He expressed recognition therein for the work of Montesquieu, but he gave his preference to Condorcet, the "first" to see "precisely" that "civilization is subject to a progressive path".[81] This was also the case in his *Cours de philosophie positive*. Comte was quick to claim that "the first and most important series of works that stands as directly destined to the final establishment of social science is [...] that of the great Montesquieu, first in his treatise on Roman politics, and especially later in his *Esprit des lois*";[82] Comte also admitted that Montesquieu contributed to the overthrow of the myth of the Great Legislator.[83] But here again he ranked Condorcet more highly and, furthermore, specified that the latter's thought was prepared by the "preceding and precious insights into the theory of human perfectibility" present in the work of Turgot.[84]

We also have his criticisms of Smith, considered an "illustrious and wise philosopher", author of an "immortal" work, but "still linked", "like all his contemporaries, even the most eminent", to "metaphysics":[85] a judgement that extends to the entire economic theory inspired by Smith, which is affected by a "fundamental vice"; namely, "having proved, as to certain matters, far from being the most important, the spontaneous and permanent tendency of human societies towards a certain necessary order, it infers that this tendency does not require to be regulated by positive institutions".[86] This theory is therefore

> an essential part of the total system of critical philosophy, which during the strictly revolutionary period carried out a task which was indispensable, although only transitory [...], it has participated in an appropriate way and nearly always very honourably in this great intellectual struggle, radically discrediting the complex of industrial politics with which the old regime had been developing since Middle Ages [...]. This purely provisional function, indeed, constitutes the main social effectiveness of this doctrine [...]. The general spirit of political economy, for anyone who has properly assessed it in the totality of writings that refer to it, leads today essentially to the assertion, as a universal dogma, of the necessary absence of every regulatory intervention.[87]

Consequently, "government is [...] no longer regarded as the head of society, destined to collect all individual activities *in a single bundle and direct them to a* common end".[88] Rulers are subjected to the supervision of the ruled: they are represented "as a natural enemy encamped in the midst of our social system, against which society needs to fortify itself by the guarantees already obtained while maintaining a permanent attitude of mistrust and defensive hostility ready to break forth at the first symptom of attack".[89] "The dogma of sovereignty of the people" prevails,[90] based on the "dogma of unlimited freedom of conscience".[91] And, where "the sovereignty of every individual reason" is proclaimed, "*there is no society*".[92]

How do you go beyond all this? There are three stages in humanity's path: once the theological stage and the metaphysical stage have been passed, there will be the positive stage, in which there will no longer be "arbitrary theology, or the divine right of kings, and the arbitrary metaphysics, or the sovereignty of the people";[93] and the "government by measures replaces government by men".[94] This is the foreshadowing of an a-economic and a-political society, which will come into being regardless of the will of each.

To use Popper's terminology, we are here confronted by an "unconditional historical prophecy":[95] there is in fact no indication of what makes the achievement of the final goal possible; and the inevitability of this hinges exclusively on the assertion made by Comte, who is the sole guarantor of the destiny in gestation.

In Comte's mind, there was indeed something different. The new order would not have been established without the intervention of human will. It was to have been a *deliberate construction*, entrusted to "scientific men", the only ones to be depositaries of an "organic doctrine", capable of directing our lives, and the only group which could therefore be "the head of society, as the guide and agent of general activity".[96] This is an idea which is underpinned by a coarse form of gnoseological absolutism. Comte stated:

> In astronomy, physics, chemistry and physiology there is no such a thing as liberty of conscience; that is to say everyone would deem it absurd not to place confidence in the principles established for these sciences by competent thinkers. If the case is different in politics, this arises from the circumstance that, the old principles having been abandoned while the new are yet unformed, established principles during this interregnum do not in a just sense exist. But to convert this transitory fact into an absolute and eternal dogma and treat it as a fundamental principle, evidently amounts to a proclamation that society should always continue deprived of any general doctrinal basis. It must be admitted that such a notion justly deserves the charge of anarchy brought against it by the ablest defenders of the theological system.[97]

The premise of ignorance and fallibility, on which the social sciences were born, is thus uprooted. Not everyone knows everything, but a sophocratic reign is possible. It is enough to rely on the "scientific men", who have the attribute of omniscience. The problem of unintended consequences is erased;[98] and every social phenomenon must be interpreted in the light of the plan of history, of which the *wise* are the sole custodians.

Therefore, there is a total discontinuity with the major acquisitions of the eighteenth century. But that legacy was not lost. It was preserved thanks to Herbert Spencer, who took up the assumption of ignorance and fallibility from which the social sciences were born. As he wrote: "the sincere man of science [...] becomes by each new inquiry more profoundly convinced that the Universe is an insoluble problem [...]. In all directions, his investigations eventually bring him face to face with the unknowable; and he ever more clearly perceives it to be unknowable."[99]

Spencer reminded us that he had first addressed the issue of the birth of moral rules in *Social Statics*, a work that was published in late 1850, and dated 1851;[100] and he declared that he had always made use of the theory of "sympathy".[101] He had in fact posed the following question: if every man is driven to "assert and defend his own liberty of action", "whence comes our perception of the right of others"?[102] To which he had answered:

> The way to a solution of this difficulty has been opened by Adam Smith in his *Theory of Moral Sentiments*. It is the aim of that work to show that the proper regulation of our conduct to one another is secured by means of a faculty whose function it is to excite in each being the emotions displayed by surrounding ones [...] a faculty, in short, which we commonly call sympathy.[103]

In other words, the identification of the expectations of others is what allows the co-adaptation of actions, mutual benefit and social cooperation.[104]

Rules and social institutions "have arisen without the devising of any one"; they are the unintended outcome of the "individual efforts of citizens severally to satisfy their own wants".[105] This idea runs through the entirety of Spencer's sociological work. Again, following the path marked out by Smith (in this case, through his assertions in the *Wealth of Nations*), it is also affirmed with regard to the division of labour:

> While each citizen has been pursuing his individual welfare, and none taking thought about division of labour, or indeed conscious of the need for it, division of labour has yet been even becoming more complete. It has been doing this slowly and silently; scarcely any having observed it until quite modern times.[106]

Moreover, Spencer explained that the "genesis" of simple governments, as well as compound governments, is determined by the "conditions" to which the ruled and rulers co-adapt their actions and not by the "intentions" of someone;[107] he understood that social rules and institutions can change indefinitely,[108] as a result of the continuous "re-adjustment" of individual projects;[109] he highlighted that "social progress is not linear";[110] he saw in social cooperation an ateleological process; he combated the illusion that society was created *ex nihilo*, so that it was "artificially" assembled by some conscious, divine and/or human will;[111] and he consistently emphasized that, if in the biological organism "consciousness is concentrated in a small part of the aggregate", while

> in the other [the social organism] it is diffused throughout the aggregate: all the units possess the capacity for happiness and misery, if not in equal degree, still in degrees that approximate [...], *there is no social sensorium*, the welfare of the aggregate, considered apart from that of the units, is not an end to be sought. The society exists for the benefit of its members, not its members for the benefit of the society.[112]

5.4 APPENDIX: SPENCER AND DARWIN

To remain in the exclusive territory of the social sciences, Spencer was not solely indebted to Smith. He was influenced by Erasmus Darwin, who had in turn benefited from Hume's teaching. He found in Mackintosh a confirmation of significant parts of what had been developed in Edinburgh.[113] He reckoned with Thomas R. Malthus' *Essay on the Principle of Population*.[114] And in any case he understood that evolutionary theory had had its first application in the field of the phenomena of social life.

Charles Darwin also owed a debt towards the social sciences. We have his admission of having found inspiration in Malthus:

> In October 1838, that is, fifteen months after I had begun my systematic enquiry, I happened to read for amusement Malthus on *Population*, and being well prepared to appreciate the struggle for existence which everywhere goes on from long-continued observation of habits of animals and plants, it at once struck me that under these circumstances favourable variations tend to be to be preserved, and unfavourable ones to be destroyed.[115]

This coincides with what is usually repeated. But it should be added that his grandfather, Erasmus, was the most immediate intermediary with the work of Hume, which he had moreover known directly.[116] As for his relationship with Smith's works, one needs to bear in mind that he had knowledge of the *History of Astronomy*, the essay in which the Scotsman first posed the problem of unintended consequences;[117] one should also recall that, not unlike Spencer, he focused on "*sympathy*" (as a principle by which to achieve the co-adaptation of actions) and on the division of labour;[118] and one should also be consider that he benefited from the text in which Dugald Stewart commemorated Smith.[119] Nor is the relationship with Mackintosh to be overlooked.[120]

Spencer and Darwin thus benefited from what the social sciences had produced prior to their works. Both also "influenced each other to some degree".[121] In truth, Darwin denied that he had been inspired in any way by Spencer; he explicitly said he did not think "of having profited" in his work from "Spencer's writings".[122] But this is at odds with the way their intellectual paths unfolded, which show clear points of intersection. Spencer had understood that social life is dominated by the evolutionary principle; and he proposed to extend its application to the world of nature. If in society change is due to the continuous re-adaptation of individual plans, on which the possibility of obtaining the cooperation of others depends, what does the evolutionary principle operate with outside human society?

That such was Spencer's programme of research is evidenced by the work he published prior to the publication of the *Origin of Species*. It suffices, among other works, to mention *Social Statics* (1851), *The Development Hypothesis* (1852), *Theory of Population* (1852), *The Universal Postulate* (1853), *The Genesis of Science* (1854), *Progress: its Law and Cause* (1857). As we know from his correspondence, Spencer sent his essays to Darwin, who thanked him and expressed himself in the following terms (in a letter dated 25 November 1858) with reference to *The Development Hypothesis*:

> Your remarks on the general argument of the so-called development theory seem to me admirable. I am at present preparing an abstract of a larger work on the changes of species; but I treat the subject simply as a naturalist, and not from a general point of view, otherwise, in my opinion, your argument [...] might have been quoted by me with great advantage.[123]

This judgement is entirely understandable. For Spencer's essay contains a vigorous affirmation of the "theory of evolution".[124] But the answer to the question of how the evolutionary principle operates outside society was provided by Darwin, through the idea of "natural selection".

Even after the publication of the *Origin of Species*, Darwin continued to closely follow Spencer's work and express his esteem for the author. In a letter sent on 10 December 1866 to Joseph D. Hooker, he wrote:

> I have now read the last number [of the *Principles of Biology*]. I do not know whether to think it better than the previous number, but it is wonderfully clever, and I dare say mostly true. I feel rather mean when I read him [Spencer]: I could bear, and rather enjoy feeling that he was twice as ingenious and clever as myself, but when I feel that he is about a dozen times my superior, even in the master art of wriggling, I feel aggrieved.[125]

When he received the entire volume of the work, addressing Spencer directly, Darwin wrote: "In many parts of your *Principles of Biology* I was fairly astonished at the prodigality of your original views. Most of the chapters furnished suggestions for whole volumes of future researches."[126] In a subsequent letter of 15 March 1870, addressed to E. Ray Lankester, Darwin further stated: "It has also pleased me to see how thoroughly you appreciate H. Spencer [...]; I suspect that hereafter he will be looked at as by far the greatest living philosopher in England."[127] Finally, it is worth remembering what Darwin wrote in his autobiography. Although he there made it public that he did not find Spencer a "particularly" pleasant person, he reiterated that he had always found his "conversation" with him "very interesting";[128] and added: "After reading any of his books, I generally feel enthusiastic admiration for his transcendent talents".[129]

Consideration and estimation were not one way. Spencer acknowledged that, "up to the time at which the papers by Mr. Darwin and Mr. Wallace, read before the Linnaean Society, had become known" to him, he "held that the sole cause of organic evolution is the inheritance of functionally-produced modifications";[130] and specified: "The *Origin of Species* made it clear to me that I was wrong; and that the larger part of the facts cannot be due to any such cause."[131] And there is more. Since there is a reference to what Darwin later called "natural selection" on a page of the essay on the *Theory of Population*,[132] Spencer blamed himself for not having been able to draw the due conclusions at the right time.[133]

There is, however, one point on which Spencer claimed a primacy for his work. Seeing the expression "Darwinian ethics" gaining currency, he recalled out how extensive his work had been in the field of social theory, starting with *Social Statics*.[134] But he harboured no illusions. He considered any clarification "hopeless";[135] and, what is more significant here, he once again pointed out that evolutionary theory had had its first application in the study of social phenomena.[136]

NOTES

1. Burke (1757), p. 21, emphasis added.
2. See Hume's letter to Smith of 12 April 1759 (Greig, 1932, vol. 1, pp. 303–306) and Burke's letter to Smith of 10 September of the same year (Smith, [1740–1790] 1976–83e, pp. 46–47). The *Annual Register* was a review of major political and cultural events, published by Burke with the publisher Dodsley. The *Wealth of Nations* also received a highly laudatory review in the *Annual Register*; but it is not possible to determine whether the author of the review was Burke himself or one of his associates.
3. Prior (1891), p. 38.
4. Bisset (1800), vol. 2, p. 429.
5. During his brief stay in Scotland, in April 1784, Burke went to Edinburgh, where he was welcomed, also on behalf of the city authorities, by Smith, who was at his side at every moment of his visit. See Rae (1895), p. 388.
6. Burke ([1790] 1951), p. 153.
7. See Chapter 4, text corresponding to endnote 93.
8. Burke ([1790] 1951), p. 166.
9. Op. cit., p. 92.
10. Op. cit., p. 188.
11. Op. cit., pp. 243–244, emphasis added.
12. Op. cit., p. 84.
13. Burke (1800), p. 11. Burke's statement is nothing more than a revival of Smith's "invisible hand".
14. It is no coincidence that, in times closer to us, Merton (1968, p. 1120) wrote that "the *distinctive* intellectual contributions of the sociologist are found primarily in the study of unintended consequences (among which are latent functions) of social practice".
15. Burke ([1790] 1951), p. 58.
16. Ibid.
17. Op. cit., p. 121.
18. Ibid.

19. Aristotle (B), 1292a.
20. Ibid.
21. Ibid.
22. Ibid.
23. Burke (1791), p. 97.
24. It was Dunn (1941) who referred to Smith and Burke as "complementary contemporaries".
25. Constant (1907), pp. 10–11. Constant defined his Edinburgh experience as "the most pleasant of his whole life" (op. cit., p. 10).
26. Zemek (1987), p. 50.
27. Ibid.
28. Ibid. Fontana (1988, p. 33) went as far as to say that the 1806 *Principes* "can be read as a close commentary on Smith's *Wealth of Nations*". Fontana (1991, p. 39) further stated: "Most of the things Constant wrote during his life were always closer to the historical and sociological vision of Montesquieu and Adam Smith, the two authors he most admired and which he most frequently quoted in his works." It is however necessary to point out that Constant (1980, pp. 304–305) considered that Montesquieu possessed, on the subject of political economy, only "superficial notions" and that it was therefore necessary to "avoid taking him as a guide"; one can add, as we already know, the criticism levelled by Constant himself, in the area of political analysis, against Montesquieu, because of the fact that the latter attributed the "difference to the republic and the monarchy", while "it ought [...] to be attributed to the opposed spirit of ancient and modern times" (see Chapter 4, endnote 57). On the Scottish influence on Constant, see also Wood (1986, pp. 151–166) and De Luca (2003, pp. 112–113; 2007, p. 32, footnote 8).
29. Constant (1980), p. 68.
30. Ibid.
31. Ibid. In later years, considering the work of Filangieri, Constant (1822, p. 36) tackled the problem once again. He criticized the Italian thinker for considering the legislator "as a being apart, above the rest of men, necessarily better and more enlightened than others". He added that the author of *La scienza della legislazione*, "becoming excited over a phantom his own imagination had created", attributed it a power he rarely thought of limiting (ibid.); and he concluded that, according to the Italian thinker, one might deem that law falls "from the sky, pure and infallible, without the need to resort to intermediaries, whose errors distort it, whose personal calculations disfigure it, whose vices score it and make it perverse [...] the law is the work of men [... and] the work does not merit greater confidence than its makers" (op. cit., p. 39).
32. Constant (1980), p. 227.
33. Op. cit., p. 130.
34. Op. cit., p. 271.
35. Op. cit., p. 68.
36. Op. cit., p. 310. For further clarification, it is useful to quote two passages by Constant. The first is taken from the 1806 *Principes*: "Since the action undertaken in the name of all is necessarily, whether one likes it or not, the action of one or few, it follows that, by conferring the power upon all, it is not at all true that it is given to none. Conversely, it is given to those who act in the name of all" (op. cit., pp. 33–34). The second passage is from the 1815 *Principes*: "as soon as sovereignty has to make use of the power it holds or, in other words, as soon as

it is necessary to proceed to the practical organization of power [...], the action undertaken in the name of all is unavoidably, whether we like it or not, the action of a single individual, or a few individuals, and it therefore comes about that by subjecting himself to all [...], each submits himself to those who act in the name of all" (Constant, [1815] 1872a, pp. 10–11).

37. Constant (1980), p. 468.
38. Ibid.
39. Op. cit., p. 24.
40. Op. cit., p. 534.
41. One can therefore understand the criticisms levelled against Bentham, whom Constant reproached in particular for not seeing that "a right is a principle; utility is only a result" (op. cit., p. 60).
42. Burke ([1790] 1951), p. 216.
43. For an extensive discussion of Smith's influence on Constant, see Infantino (2019), pp. 49–84. It is also important to point out that the expression "interest rightly understood" will later be used for the same purposes by Tocqueville ([1835–1840] 1994, vol. 2, p. 123), on whom one can clearly trace the influence of Constant and also of Guizot, of whom Tocqueville had been a pupil at the Sorbonne. Using the theory of unintended consequences, Guizot ([1828] 1885) explained in particular the birth of individual freedom of choice in Europe. On the relationship between the so-called "doctrinaires" and Tocqueville, see De Sanctis (1986, p. 23); for a more general treatment of doctrinarian liberalism, inspired by British evolutionism, cf. the classic work by Diez del Corral (1956), which develops an idea of Ortega y Gasset's ([1930] 1946–83g, pp. 123–129).
44. Infantino (2020a), pp. 5–18.
45. Hayek (1960), p. 29.
46. Popper (1966), vol. 2, p. 93.
47. Ibid., emphasis added.
48. Mill ([1843] 1892), p. 531.
49. Bentham ([1823] (1907), pp. 13–15.
50. Mill ([1843] 1892), p. 546. The passage is also included in Mill ([1844] 1967), p. 322.
51. Russell (1956), p. 118.
52. Ibid.
53. Mill ([1848] 1965), vol. 2, p. 754.
54. Mill ([1843] 1892), p. 565.
55. Halévy ([1901] 1972), p. 487. This should have prevented Halévy from seeing in Bentham "the disciple of Hume and Adam Smith" (op. cit., p. 142).
56. For a more extensive discussion, see Infantino (2008), pp. 69–111 and 146–152.
57. Schumpeter (1954), p. 531.
58. Jevons ([1871] 1888), p. 37.
59. Ibid.
60. Walras (1896), vol. 1, p. iv.
61. Op. cit., vol. 2, p. 459.
62. On social "constructivism", see Hayek (1978), pp. 3–22. The ambition to intentionally establish the social order contains a mechanistic idea that dates back, beyond Newton, to Descartes and had a powerful influence on English utilitarianism and French positivism. Guyau (1885, p. 5) rightly wrote: "Bentham's disciples compared their master to Descartes. '*Donnez moi la matière et le mouvement*', said Descartes, '*et je ferai le monde*'. Bentham could say, in his turn,

'Give me human affections, joy and sorrow, pain and pleasure, and I shall create a moral world. I shall produce not only justice, but also generosity, patriotism, philanthropy, and all the amiable and sublime virtues in their purity.'"
63. Jaffé (1976), p. 521.
64. Ibid.
65. Menger ([1883] 1996), p. 137. Since the publication of his *Grundsätze der Volkswirtschaftslehre*, the Austrian economist called attention to money as an institution born without prior programming (Menger, [1871] 1994). The issue of the unintended origin of social institutions was subsequently discussed extensively in *Untersuchungen über die Methode der Socialwissenschaften, und der politischen Ökonomie insbesondere* (Menger, [1883] 1996). Menger also dedicated a more specific study, *Geld*, to the birth of money (Menger, [1892] 2002).
66. Kauder (1965), p. 100. See also Antonelli (1953). As is well known, Menger's reservations with regard to Walras were later turned into Hayek's (1949, pp. 33–56) criticism of the theory of general economic equilibrium. This criticism highlights, among other things, the absence of the social process as an indispensable tool for co-adapting individual plans. That is: Walras worked on the assumption that actors, if not omniscient, possess the knowledge of the *relevant data*. This makes the process of adjusting plans unnecessary, because each operator knows in advance what he can and cannot do on the market. Equilibrium already exists, it is not necessary to achieve it.
67. Hayek (1949), p. 4, note 3.
68. See Preface, endnote 11.
69. Menger ([1883] 1996), p. 153.
70. Op. cit., p. 154.
71. Op. cit., p. 156.
72. Hayek (1969), p. 103. As an illustration of Savigny's position, it is worth quoting the following passage: "all this effort to improve the legal conditions by sweeping stroke from above, which aims to govern everything more and more, is nothing but another extension of the unfortunate trend that has characterized public life for so long, namely the tendency to want *to govern everything, and to govern more and more* [...]. The supporters of this view think that the world can be greatly improved by orders and regulations. Though their intentions may be very noble, most of those who embitter our lives with excessive regulations claim they are doing it for our own good, and expect our gratitude" (Savigny, 1816, p. 2). For further clarification, it is useful to add what Ehrlich ([1917] 1928, p. 84) wrote: "Burke, Savigny and Puchta [...] see, and this has always been underestimated, under the idea of a people or a nation the same thing that we today call society in opposition to the State, understood as territorial sovereignty." It is also important to bear in mind that, in *Untersuchungen*, Menger ([1883] 1996, p. 183, note 132) quoted Spencer's *Descriptive Sociology* and, in *Geld* (Menger, [1892] 2002, p. 89, note 4), referred to *Principles of Sociology* also by Spencer, who never concealed his debts towards Smith. This will be discussed in the next section.
73. See Menger ([1891] 2016). What Smith ([1776] 1976–83b, vol. 1, p. 47) wrote precisely was: "Labour [...] is the real measure of the exchangeable value of all commodities."
74. For a broader discussion of Menger's criticism of Smith, see Cubeddu (2018), pp. 13–33.
75. See Chapter 2, endnote 66.

76. Hume ([1739–1740] 1930), vol. 2, p. 36.
77. See Chapter 4, endnote 86.
78. Smith ([1776] 1976–83b), vol. 2, p. 660.
79. Significantly, Kirzner (1992, pp. 134–136) wrote that it was Menger's influence that led Mises and Hayek to underscore the distance between Austrian marginalism and the other currents of neoclassical economics. Obviously, as Hayek (1949, p. 47, note 12) himself emphasized, utilitarianism in the strict sense leads economists towards the pure logic of choice; this has already been flagged in the preface. And yet, in order to explain social phenomena, it is necessary to resort to the analysis of the institutional *habitat* and the process that the actors give life to. This had been grasped well beforehand by Small (1907, p. 4). For a more extensive discussion of the point, see Infantino (2020b, p. 230).
80. Comte ([1830–1842] 1970c), p. 201, footnote 1.
81. Comte ([1822] 1970a), p. 109.
82. Comte ([1830–1842] 1970c), p. 193.
83. Op. cit., p. 195.
84. Op. cit., p. 201.
85. Op. cit., p. 213.
86. Comte ([1826] 1970b), p. 209, footnote 2.
87. Comte ([1830–1842] 1970c), pp. 217–218.
88. Comte ([1822] 1970a), p. 52.
89. Ibid.
90. Op. cit., p. 53.
91. Op. cit., p. 52.
92. Op. cit., p. 53, emphasis added.
93. Op. cit., p. 103.
94. Op. cit., p. 102.
95. Popper (1991), pp. 336–346.
96. Comte ([1822] 1970a), p. 52.
97. Op. cit., p. 53.
98. Therefore, it is no surprise that Comte (op. cit., p. 91) stated: "A superficial philosophy, which would make this world a scene of miracles, has immensely exaggerated the influence of chance [...]. All sensible men in our time admit that chance plays only a very small part." The consequence of this is that every negative event, even if unintentionally produced by "scientific men", must not be attributed to the inability to control all social variables, but to the will of some *enemy* that lurks in society.
99. Spencer (1857), p. 485. As we know, Spencer then dedicated the first part of the *First Principles* to the subject (Spencer, [1862] 1887, pp. 3–123).
100. Spencer ([1884] 1978), vol. 1, p. 25.
101. Op. cit., p. 24.
102. Spencer ([1851] 1995), p. 89.
103. Ibid.
104. Spencer ([1879] 1907), p. 120.
105. Spencer (1860), p. 92.
106. Op. cit., pp. 91–92. Spencer (1852, p. 20) had already made use of the idea of division of labour. He had in particular argued that it makes it possible to improve living conditions.
107. Spencer ([1877–1896] 1906), vol. 2, p. 395.
108. Spencer ([1884] 1978), vol. 1, p. 24.

109. Spencer (1873), p. 346.
110. Spencer ([1877–1896] 1906), vol. 3, p. 331.
111. Spencer (1860), pp. 90–91. This is what Spencer said at length: "Sir James Mackintosh got great credit for the saying that 'constitutions are not made but grow' [...]. Such a conception could not indeed fail to be startling when let fall in the midst of a system of thought to which it was utterly alike [...], things were explained on the hypothesis of manufacture, rather than that of growth [...], in harmony with such ideas, societies were tacitly assumed to be arranged thus or thus by direct interposition of Providence; or by the regulations of law-makers; or by both. Yet that societies are not artificially put together, is truth so manifest that it seems wonderful men should have ever overlooked it [...]. You need but a look at the changes going around, or observe social organization in its leading peculiarities, to see that these are neither supernatural, nor are determined by the wills of individual men" (ibid.).
112. Spencer ([1877–1896] 1906), vol. 1, p. 461, emphasis added. This shows that Coser's observation (1977, p. 99) that Spencer failed to reconcile "his individualism and his organicism" is misplaced. Dwelling on it is equivalent to making what is already clear murky. The fact that Spencer denied society the possibility of having a collective "sensorium" indicates that his organicism is only an analogy, the use of which is limited and exclusively instrumental. We need to ask ourselves, following Weber's method once again, whether Spencer's explanation of social phenomena, stripped of its analogy, can stand. And what is said in the text provides an unequivocally positive response. For an analysis, from the perspective adopted herein, of the works of Durkheim, Simmel and Weber and the relationship of the latter two with the Austrian School of Economics, see Infantino (1998, pp. 57–130). As for Pareto's sociology, see Infantino (2020a, pp. 181–218).
113. Spencer (1860), pp. 90–91.
114. On the relations between Daniel Malthus, Thomas' father, and Hume, see Greig (1932), vol. 2, pp. 23–25 and 33.
115. Darwin ([1887] 1958), p. 120. On the influence of Malthus' essay on Darwin, see Vorzimmer (1972, pp. 4 and 8). For the instances where Malthus is mentioned in Darwin's annotations, see Gruber and Barrett (1974).
116. See Chapter 3, note 106, containing some excerpts from Hume's *Dialogues on Natural Religion*, which certainly did not escape Erasmus Darwin's attention. See also Darwin ([1871] 1896, p. 109, footnote 23) and Gruber and Barrett (1974) for Darwin's personal notes.
117. Gruber and Barrett (1974), p. 302.
118. For the principle of *"sympathy"*, see Darwin ([1871] 1896, pp. 106–107), who was also aware of what had been written on the subject by Burke (Gruber and Barrett, 1974, p. 318). As far as the division of labour is concerned, the expression was used several times; more precisely, Darwin recognized that "even at a remote period" humans "practised some division of labour" (Darwin, [1871] 1896, p. 127).
119. Gruber and Barrett (1974, p. 286), where more details on Smith's influence can be found. Dennett (1995, p. 73) succinctly stated: "Had Darwin not had the benefit of being born into a mercantile world that had already created its Adam Smith and its Thomas Malthus, he would not have been in position to find ready-made pieces he could put together into a new, value-added product."

120. Darwin ([1887] 1958), p. 55.; ([1871] 1896), p. 97. See the various references in Gruber and Barrett (1974).
121. Coser (1977), p. 110.
122. Darwin ([1887] 1958), p. 109.
123. F. Darwin (1887), vol. 2, p. 141. Darwin ([1859] 1871, p. 20) referred to Spencer's early writings in the *Origin of Species*. Opening a collection of his essays with *The Development Hypothesis*, Spencer noted: "Brief though it is, I place this essay before the rest, partly because [...] it came first in order of time, but chiefly because it came first in order of thought and struck the keynote of all that was to follow" (Spencer, 1891, vol. 1, p. 1).
124. Among other things, we find the following statement: "Even could the supporters of the *development hypothesis* merely show that the origination of species by the process of modification is conceivable, they would be in a better position than their opponents. But they can do much more than this. They can show that the process of modification has effected, and is effecting, decided changes in all organisms" (Spencer, 1891, vol. 1, p. 3).
125. F. Darwin (1887), vol. 3, pp. 55–56.
126. F. Darwin and Seward (1903), vol. 2, p. 442.
127. F. Darwin (1887), vol. 3, p. 120.
128. Darwin ([1887] 1958), p. 108.
129. Ibid.
130. Spencer (1904), vol. 2, p. 50.
131. Ibid. Meldola (1910, p. 7) wrote in this connection: "The effect of the publication of the *Origin of Species* upon the mind of an evolutionist of such pronounced views as Spencer is an interesting episode in the history of his work. With scientific candour, he at once admitted the cogency of natural selection. Up to that time organic evolution had been for him, tacitly if not avowedly, Lamarckism – the only mechanism of development then known." In this regard, it is therefore useful to recall what Popper (1974, p. 149) wrote: "There are three senses of the verb 'to learn' which have been insufficiently distinguished by learning theorists: 'to discover'; 'to imitate'; 'to make habitual'. All three may be regarded as form of discovery, and all three operate with trial-and-error methods [...]. In all these different ways of learning or of acquiring or producing knowledge the method is Darwinian rather than Lamarckian: it is selection rather than instruction by repetition. (But we should not overlook the fact that Lamarckism is a kind of approximation to Darwinism, and that the products of selection therefore often look as if there were products of Lamarckian adaptation, of instruction through repetition: Darwinism, we can say, simulates Lamarckism)." On Spencer, see also Morganti (2015), pp. 99–133 and the extensive bibliography indicated therein.
132. Spencer (1852), p. 34.
133. Spencer (1904), vol. 1, p. 390. See also Spencer ([1864] 1886), vol. 2, p. 500.
134. Spencer ([1884] 1978), vol. 1, p. 25.
135. Op. cit., p. 26.
136. Ibid.

6. Additional considerations

> It is perhaps scarcely necessary to add that Evolution as a philosophical principle does not stand or fall with the proof or disproof of Natural Selection as a theory of species formation. (Raphael Meldola)

As we have seen in the preceding pages, the birth of the social sciences was accompanied by the use of an evolutionary conception of the phenomena produced by intersubjective interaction. The first condition for this had been to abandon the idea that behind social events there lies an ordering mind (human and/or divine), to whose unstoppable will every event could be traced. Thus, the way was opened to the attempt to understand that rules and institutions originate, without any prior planning by human beings or higher entities, from the need to make social cooperation possible; and this is the direct answer to the problem of the insufficiency of the knowledge and resources of each.

Precisely because social norms are such only if they guarantee cooperation, society is the place where individuals are released from the "struggle for survival", as it is currently understood in in the realm of nature. Even when competition results in personal antagonism, social actors measure themselves, at least in the short and medium term, in relation to their ability to be better in embodying existing social models. And, in the long run, when changes occur in lifestyles, production combinations, ways to cover old and new needs, that antagonism is resolved through the promptness with which each actor grasps the cultural "variations" that most adequately meet the needs of social cooperation. Since change is the result of a process to which we contribute, but whose outcome we are not capable of foreseeing, we can only benefit if we know how to respond to it promptly.[1]

Acquisitions in the social sciences benefited the work of Spencer and Darwin. Being a scholar of social phenomena, Spencer well knew that life as it takes place in society is very different from the way it takes place in nature; human beings cooperate because the game they participate in is a positive-sum one:[2] the concepts developed to explain what happens in the sphere of nature are therefore not transferable to the social sphere.

For his part, Darwin wanted, as he declared, to be a simple naturalist; however, he too was aware of the differences between the two territories. Some of his statements are worth examining with attention. He initially wrote:

> Man in the rudest state in which he now exists is the most dominant animal that has ever appeared on this earth. He has spread more widely that any other highly organised form: and all others have yielded before him. He manifestly owes this immense superiority to his intellectual faculties, to *his social habits*, which lead him *to aid and defend his fellows*.[3]

Darwin then added: "The small strength and speed of man, his want of natural weapons [...] are more than counterbalanced, firstly, by his intellectual powers, through which he has formed for himself weapons, tools [...] and, secondly, by his social *qualities which lead him to give and receive aid from his fellow-men.*"[4] Hence the conclusion:

> As man advances in civilisation [...], the simplest reason would tell each individual that he ought to extend his social [... sentiments] and sympathies to all the members of the same nation, though personally unknown to him. This point being once reached, there is only an artificial barrier to prevent his sympathies extending to the men of all nations and races.[5]

And yet this was not enough to prevent the birth of "social Darwinism", the insertion, that is, into the field of the social sciences, precisely by scholars of these disciplines, of categories applicable to nature but not to society. There was a reversal of roles. If originally it was the social sciences that provided ideas for the study of nature, later acquisitions from nature were applied to society. Paraphrasing Raphael Meldola, social life was interpreted in the light of "natural selection":[6] "a lasting disservice" inflicted "to the advance of the theory of cultural evolution".[7]

Exemplary, however, was the position of Thomas H. Huxley, who wrote that the *evolution of society* is "a process of an essentially different character" from that "which brings about the evolution of species"; just as it is different from what would be realized if there were an authority in charge of selection.[8] Huxley laid particular emphasis on the fact that the social process tends to ensure for every member of society, rather than the means for survival, a certain standard of living. The reason this happens is not mysterious. While the "animal cannot escape its repertoire of natural acts", "because it is one" with nature, man "invents and carries out a second repertoire of acts: he lights fires, builds houses, cultivates fields and manufactures cars", he interposes between himself and his surroundings a "new nature, a supernature", constituted by the specifically social dimension.[9]

It is no coincidence that Leslie A. White said:

> One of the most popular formulas of interpretation of human behaviour is that of "human nature". People behave as they do, have the institutions, beliefs, attitudes, games [...] that surround them because "it is human nature". And incidentally, most people – however much they may be willing to admit their ignorance in other respects – usually feel that they "understand human nature". The human mind and organism are so constituted, according to this view, as to make certain kinds of response simply and directly forthcoming. One has only to know human nature to understand society and culture and to predict the course of development. The fallacy or illusion here is, of course, that what one takes for "human nature" is not natural at all but cultural [...]. Much of what is commonly called "human nature" is merely culture thrown against a screen of nerves, glands, sense organs, muscles.[10]

It follows that

> to label "biological" the formation of the tradition of morals, law, money, even of the mind, abuses language and misunderstands theory. Our genetic inheritance may determine what we are capable of learning but certainly not what tradition is there to learn. What is [...] not transmitted by genes is not a biological phenomenon.[11]

Any of our actions must be planned, presented to others and implemented through the "third world", that universe of shared symbols and models (starting from language), which is the element that humanly connects us to others and makes social cooperation possible.[12]

It is therefore an "ethical process", the objective of which is not exclusion, but inclusion or, more precisely, better inclusion.[13] Huxley added: "What is often called the struggle for existence in society (I plead guilty to having used the term too loosely myself) is a contest", which makes social cooperation more advantageous.[14] Success is determined by qualities such as "energy, industry, intellectual capacity, tenacity of purpose" and the ability to understand the expectations of others;[15] the process is not the tool by means of which to determine the "survival of the fittest", but a means to establish how cooperation can lead to the improvement of living conditions for as many people as possible.[16]

Thus, the reason why cultural evolutionism needs the "rule of law" becomes clear. It delimits the boundaries between actions. It prevents each actor from harming others, it prevents each of us, that is, from doing his worst when he is "at his worst";[17] and leaves the decision regarding the content of the action to individual freedom. It is a situation in which, as Dugald Stewart wrote, respect for the law is "interesting to every member of the community: and more especially to those whose personal insignificance leaves them no encouragement, but what they derive from general spirit" of the law.[18] Legal and formal equality and the consequent lack of a compulsory hierarchy of ends make it possible to broaden the scope of cooperation as far as possible and to increase the volume of social exchanges. Therefore, (as we have repeatedly emphasized) this establishes an extensive process of exploration of the unknown and correction of errors, which mobilizes knowledge and resources dispersed within society. Those who are the first to adopt winning models derive immediate advantages, which they necessarily share with others; no one, in any case, is deprived of the opportunity to follow the example.[19]

Consequently, it must be understood that inter-individual exchange, voluntary cooperation, that is, is nothing more than a "peace treaty" and that "both exchange and regulated exchange" arose "together" as a unitary fact.[20] Inspired by Spencer's sociology, Georg Simmel wrote:

> robbery, and perhaps the gift, appear to be the most primitive stages of change in ownership, the advantage lying completely on one side and the burden falling completely on the other. When the stage of exchange appears as the form of change in ownership [...], then this would be evidence of the greatest progress than mankind could have made.[21]

It is the situation in which the "mere one-sidedness of advantage" disappears;[22] and this constitutes a real ethicization of our life condition.[23]

As Huxley pointed out, it was an unfortunate idea to introduce into the social sciences, after evolutionism established itself outside them, concepts such as "natural selection", "struggle for existence", or "survival of the most suitable". More precisely, it was a mistake; and this for three types of reason: (a) because it was interaction and co-adaptation of actions that humanized us; (b) because the "decisive factor", in social evolution, "is not the selection of the physical and inheritable properties of the individuals, but the selection by imitation of successful institutions and habits";[24] and (c) because social cooperation, if it were not a positive-sum game, would not be such or, rather, would not take place. Faced with this, "social Darwinism" remained totally blind. Consistently argued, it leads to universal war. In fact, there is no reason why "existential struggle" should not also take place within social formations (nations or races) to which the supporters of this theory direct their preferences:[25] if social exchange is a positive-sum game, it always is; if it is not, it never is.

There is still one point to focus on. As we know, the unintended results of our actions necessarily derive from our condition of ignorance and fallibility (and require us to recognize that the social process can only have an ateleological character). However, it often occurs that attention to the problem of unintended consequences is presented as a form of indulgence towards political conservatism; and it is therefore said that the Scottish Enlightenment thinkers and their followers deserve to be "rebuked" for not being aware of the possible use, in a conservative sense, of the theory of unintended outcomes.[26] This takes on an even more severe tone when, as in the case of Albert O. Hirschman, it is admitted that unintended consequences are the very *"raison d'être"* of social science, but it is added that the "perverse effects", which are nothing more than unintended consequences of a negative nature, constitute "a basic characteristic of reactionary rhetoric".[27]

Such criticisms do not touch the inescapable fact that unintended outcomes are the product of the human condition; to be aware of them is simply to be ready to accept their advantages and to correct the errors on which the disadvantages depend. It also needs to be said that the proponents of cultural evolutionism, recognizing the unstoppable nature of the social process, do not at all aim at preventing change; and it can be added, with regard to the political use of a theory or a use other than that indicated by its formulator or formulators, that there is nothing that can prevent it. As Weber wrote, "in the press, in public meetings, in associations, in essays" and in every manifestation of public life, each "can and should do what his God or daemon demands".[28] But this cannot lead us to deny that unintended consequences are the object of the social sciences and that their study, showing us how it is possible to turn our backs on the myth of the sole (human and/or divine) decision-maker, has led (and leads) to an increase in our rationality.

NOTES

1. Hayek (1960), p. 60.
2. Spencer ([1879] 1907), p. 120.
3. Darwin ([1871] 1896), p. 48, emphasis added.
4. Op. cit., p. 64, emphasis added.
5. Op. cit., p. 122. The idea of cooperation with unknown persons is already found in Smith; see the text quoted in endnote 99 in Chapter 4. It is no coincidence that Patten (1899, p. xxiii) wrote: "Darwin was the last of the economists and the first of the biologists."
6. Meldola (1910), p. 4.
7. Hayek (1988), p. 27. Hayek (1988, p. 23) had already stated that a social theorist of the nineteenth century, who was worthy of the name, would not need to borrow the idea of evolution from Darwin. Unfortunately, there were those who needed it; and it produced those conceptions that under the name of 'social Darwinism' have since been responsible for the diffidence with which social scientists look at the concept of evolution.
8. Huxley (1900), p. 83.
9. Ortega y Gasset ([1939] 1946–83i), pp. 323–324.
10. White (1949), p. 149. Although White clarified that cultural models "can no more exist without men" (op. cit., p. 408), thus aiming to recognize that they are a (unintended) product of human action, he fell into the reifying temptation to attribute to culture "a life of its own" and to consider it "independently of the human species" (op. cit., p. 407).
11. Hayek (1988), p. 25. Thus, it becomes clear that the "chief error of contemporary 'sociobiology' is to suppose that language, morals, law [...] are transmitted by

the 'genetic' processes that molecular biology is now illuminating, rather than being the products of selective evolution, transmitted by imitative learning" (op. cit., p. 24). The "human mind" itself is not "something innate" in the organism, something "biologically determined"; it is "obviously a variable [... and] its variations are functions of the cultural factor rather than of the psychosomatic factor" (White, 1949, pp. 147–148). See also what was written in Chapter 4, endnote 82.

12. As is well known, the expression "third world" is Popper's. See Chapter 4, endnote 89.
13. Huxley (1900), p. 82.
14. Op. cit., p. 85. It is worth noting that Darwin himself ([1859] 1871, p. 71) stated that he used the expression "struggle for existence" in "a large and metaphorical sense". Montalenti (1990, p. 54) wrote in this regard: "The concept of selection is not necessarily linked to that of struggle for existence: an organism not well adapted to a certain environment does not prosper and ends up becoming extinct, even without being able to speak of a real struggle with other organisms of the same or another species."
15. Huxley (1900), p. 86. Huxley used "*sympathy*" in the Smithian meaning of the term (op. cit., p. 77).
16. Op. cit., p. 121. Obviously, the judge of every change is time. Darwin ([1859] 1871, pp. 87–88) significantly wrote: "How fleeting are the wishes and efforts of man! how short his time! and consequently how poor will be his results, compared with those accumulated by Nature during whole geological periods! Can we wonder, then, that Nature's productions should be far 'truer' in character than man's productions; that they should be infinitely better adapted to the most complex conditions of life, and should plainly bear the stamp of far higher workmanship?" On the obstacles that stand in the way of the process of cultural evolution, see Hayek (1988, p. 20).
17. Hayek (1949), p. 11.
18. Stewart ([1793] 1980), p. 310. It is useful here to recall what was already stated by Hesiod ([A], 276 et seq.): "this was the rule for men that Kronos' son laid down: whereas fish and beasts and flying birds would eat one another, because Right is not among them, to men he gave Right, which is much the best in practice".
19. Hayek (1978), pp. 179–190.
20. Simmel ([1900] 1978), p. 99.
21. Op. cit., p. 290. See also Spencer ([1877–1896] 1906), vol. 2, p. 83 et seq., vol. 3, p. 387 et seq.; see also Menger ([1892] 2002), pp. 60–61.
22. Simmel ([1900] 1978), p. 291.
23. Op. cit., p. 419.
24. Hayek (1960), p. 59. See also Montalenti (2009), p. 16.
25. Mises ([1922] 1981b), pp. 282–283. The term "social Darwinism" here refers to those doctrines that present social cooperation outside of certain privileged groups as a zero-sum game. For an extensive discussion of the topic, see La Vergata (2005).
26. See Ross (1987, p. xi) and Hamowy (1987, p. 13).
27. Hirschman (1991), pp. 35–36. On this issue, Hirschman and Boudon (Boudon, 1992, pp. 109–119) engaged in an intense discussion. See Fallocco (2003), pp. 3–23.
28. Weber ([1917] 1949), p. 5.

References

Acton Lord (1887), *A History of Freedom in Antiquity*, in *Selected Writings*, vol. 1, Indianapolis 1985: Liberty Fund.
Antonelli È (1953), "Léon Walras et Carl Menger á travers leur correspondence", in *Économie Appliquée*, vol. 6, pp. 269–287.
Aristotle (A), "Metaphysics", in *Works*, vol. 8, Oxford 1928: Clarendon Press.
Aristotle (B), *Politics*, Cambridge, MA 1990: Harvard University Press.
Aristotle (C), *Poetics*, London 1898: Macmillan.
Augustine (A), "Of True Religion", in *Augustine: Earlier Writings*, Philadelphia 1953: Westminster Press.
Augustine (B), *The City of God*, Edinburgh: Clark.
Bacon F. ([1624] 1925), *New Atlantis*, Girard: Haldeman-Julius.
Bacon F. ([1620] 1975), *The New Organon*, Indianapolis: Bobbs-Merrill.
Bartley W.W. III (1984), *The Retreat to Commitment*, La Salle and London: Open Court Publishing.
Bay C. (1968), *Structure of Freedom*, New York: Atheneum.
Bayle P. ([1697] 1820), *Dictionnaire historique et critique*, Desoer: Paris.
Bayle P. ([1682] 1965–70a), *Pensées diverses*, in Bayle (1965–70e), vol. 3.
Bayle P. ([1694] 1965–70b), *Continuation des pensées diverses*, in Bayle (1965–70e), vol. 3.
Bayle P. ([1683] 1965–70c), *Critique generale de l'histoire du Calvinisme*, in Bayle (1965–70e), vol. 2.
Bayle P. ([1685] 1965–70d), *Nouvelles lettres de l'auteur de la critique generale de l'histoire du Calvinisme*, in Bayle (1965–70e), vol. 2.
Bayle P. (1965–70e), *Oeuvres diverses*, Hildesheim: Georg Olms.
Becker H. (1950), *Through Values to Social Interpretation*, Durham: Duke University Press.
Bentham J. ([1823] 1907), *Introduction to the Principles of Morals and Legislation*, Oxford: Clarendon Press.
Biscardi A. (1982), *Diritto greco antico*, Milan: Giuffrè.
Bisset R. (1800), *The Life of Edmund Burke*, London: Cawthorn.
Bobbio N. (1990), *L'età dei diritti*, Torino: Einaudi.
Bonar J. (1893), *Philosophy and Political Economy*, London: Sonnenschein.
Boudon R. (1992), "È reazionaria la retorica?", in *Quaderni di Sociologia*, vol. 36, pp. 109–119.
Brega G.P. (1957), *Nota introduttiva*, in Bayle P., *Pensieri sulla cometa e Dizionario critico e storico*, Milan: Feltrinelli.
Bultrighini U. (1999), *"Maledetta democrazia". Studi su Crizia*, Alessandria: Edizioni dell'Orso.
Burckhardt J. (1900), *Griechische Kulturgeschichte*, Berlin and Stuttgart: Spemann.
Burke E. (1757), *A Philosophical Inquiry into the Origin of our Ideas of the Sublime and the Beautiful*, London: Dodsley.
Burke E. (1791), *An Appeal from the New to the Old Whigs*, London: Dodsley.

Burke E. (1800), *Thoughts and Details on Scarcity*, London: Rivington.
Burke E. ([1790] 1951), *Reflection on French Revolution*, London: Dent.
Cairnes J.E. (1873), *Essays in Political Economy*, London: Macmillan.
Cannan E. (1904), *Preface* to Smith A., *An Inquiry into the Nature and Causes of the Wealth of Nations*, London: Methuen.
Carmichael G. (1729), *Synopsis Theologiae Naturalis*, Edinburgh: Paton.
Cassirer E. ([1932] 1967), *The Question of Jean-Jacques Rousseau*, London: Indiana University Press.
Cicero (A), *De Re Pubblica*, London 1926: Heinemann; New York: Putnam.
Clark W.E. (1903), *Josiah Tucker Economist*, New York: Columbia University Press.
Colletti L. (1975), *Ideologia e società*, Rome and Bari: Laterza.
Comte A. ([1822] 1970a), *Plan des travaux scientifiques nécessaries pour réorganiser la société*, in Comte (1970d), vol. 10.
Comte A. ([1826] 1970b), *Considérations sur le pouvoir spiritual*, in Comte (1970d), vol. 10.
Comte A. ([1830–1842] 1970c), *Cours de philosophie positive*, in Comte (1970d), vol. 4.
Comte A. (1970d), *Oeuvres*, Paris: Antropos.
Constant B. (1822), *Commentaire sur l'ouvrage de Filangieri*, Paris: Dufart.
Constant B. ([1815] 1872a), *Principes de politique* (of 1815), in Constant (1872c), vol. 1.
Constant B. ([1819] 1872b), *De la liberté des anciens comparée à celle des modernes*, in Constant (1872c), vol. 2.
Constant B. (1872c), *Cours de politique constitutionelle*, Paris: Guillaumin.
Constant B. (1907), *Le cahier rouge*, Paris: Colmann-Levy.
Constant B. (1980), *Principes des politique* (of 1806), Genève: Droz.
Coser L. (1977), *Masters of Sociological Thought*, New York: Harcourt Brace Jovanovich.
Cubeddu R. (2015), "Considerazioni su Mandeville e sulla scontentezza dell'alveare", in *Il Politico*, vol. 80, pp. 115–137.
Cubeddu R. (2018), "Una pagina rimossa nella storia del liberalismo: la critica di Menger a Smith", preface to *Scambio, valore e capitale*, Torino: IBL.
Darwin C. ([1859] 1871), *On the Origin of Species by Means of Natural Selection*, New York: Appleton.
Darwin C. ([1871] 1896), *The Descent of Man, Selection in Relation to Sex*, London: Murray.
Darwin C. ([1887] 1958), *Autobiography*, in Barlow N., *The Autobiography of Charles Darwin*, London: Collins.
Darwin C. ([1879] 2003), *The Life of Erasmus Darwin*, Cambridge: Cambridge University Press.
Darwin F. (1887), *The Life and the Letters of Charles Darwin*, London: Murray.
Darwin F., Seward A.C. (1903), *More Letters of Charles Darwin*, London: Murray.
Dawkins R. (1996), *The Blind Watchmaker*, New York and London: Norton.
De Luca S. (2003), *Alle origini del liberalismo contemporaneo*, Lungro: Marco Editore.
De Luca S. (2007), *Introduzione*, in Constant B., *Princìpi di politica* (del 1806), Soveria Mannelli: Rubbettino.
Dennett D.C. (1995), *Darwin's Dangerous Idea*, London: Penguin.
De Sanctis F.M. (1986), *Tempo di democrazia*, Napoli: ESI.
Descartes R. ([1637] 1901a), "Discourse on Method", in Descartes (1901c).
Descartes R. ([1641] 1901b), "Metaphysical Meditations", in Descartes (1901c).

Descartes R. (1901c), *Discourse on Method and Metaphical Meditations*, London: Scott.
Diez del Corral L. (1956), *El liberalismo doctrinario*, Madrid: Instituto de Estudios Politicos.
Dilthey W. ([1883] 1959), *Einleitung in die Geistswissenschaften*, Stuttgart: Teubner.
Dodds M. (1929), *Les récits de voyages, sources de "L'Esprit des lois" de Montesquieu*, Paris: Champion.
Dunn W.C. (1941), "Adam Smith and Edmund Burke: Complimentary Contemporaries", in *Southern Economic Journal*, vol. 7, pp. 330–346.
Durkheim È ([1928] 1962), *Socialism*, London: Collier-Macmillan.
Durkheim È. ([1893] 1964), *The Division of Labor in Society*, New York: Free Press.
Durkheim È. ([1966] 1980), *Montesquieu and Rousseau, Forerunners of Sociology*, Ann Arbor: University of Michigan Press.
Ehrenberg V. (1951), *The People of Aristophanes*, Oxford: Blackwell.
Ehrenberg V. (1996), *From Solon to Socrates*, London: Routledge.
Ehrlich E. ([1917] 1928), *Juristische Logik*, Tübingen: Mohr.
Erasmus of Rotterdam ([1511] 1887), *The Praise of Folly*, London: Hamilton, Adams & Co.
Erasmus of Rotterdam ([1517] 1917), *The Complaint of Peace*, Chicago: Open Court.
Fallocco S. (2003), *La retorica dell'effetto perverso nella polemica tra Hirschman e Boudon*, Rome: Istituto Acton.
Felice D. (ed.) (2005), *Montesquieu e i suoi interpreti*, Pisa: Edizioni ETS.
Ferguson A. (1767), *Letter to David Hume (dated April 17th, 1767)*, National Library of Scotland, MS. 23155, no. 25.
Ferguson A. (1792), *Principles of Moral and Political Science*, London: Strahan & Cadell.
Ferguson A. ([1767] 1966), *An Essay on the History of Civil Society*, Edinburgh: Edinburgh University Press.
Fink Z.S. (1962), *The Classical Republicans*, Evanston: Northwestern University Press.
Fontana B. (1988), *Introduction*, in Constant B., *Political Writings*, Cambridge: Cambridge University Press.
Fontana B. (1991), *Benjamin Constant e il pensiero post-rivoluzionario*, Milan: Baldini & Castoldi.
Frazer J.G. (1925), *The Golden Bough*, New York: Macmillan.
Friedrich C.J. (1968), "The Evolving Theory and Practice of Totalitarian Regimes", in *Il Politico*, vol. 3, pp. 53–76.
Fustel de Coulanges N.-D. ([1864] 1877), *The Ancient City*, Boston: Lee & Shepard; New York: Dillingham.
Germani G. (1975), *Sociologia della modernizzazione*, Bari and Rome: Laterza.
Glotz G. (1929), *La cité grecque*, Paris: Albin.
Greig J.Y.T. (ed.) (1932), *The Letters of David Hume*, Oxford: Oxford University Press.
Grote G. (1867), *Plato and the Other Companions of Socrates*, London: Murray.
Gruber H.E., Barrett P.H. (1974), *Darwin on Man: A Psychological Study of Scientific Creativity*, New York: Dutton.
Guerci L. (1979), *La libertà degli antichi e la libertà dei moderni*, Napoli: Guida.
Guizot F. ([1828] 1885), *Histoire de la civilisation en Europe*, Paris: Perrin.
Guyau J.M. (1885), *La morale anglaise contemporaine*, Paris: Alcan.
Haakonssen K. (1981), *The Science of a Legislator*, Cambridge: Cambridge University Press.

Halévy É. ([1901] 1972), *The Growth of Philosophical Radicalism*, London: Faber & Faber.
Hamowy R. (1968), "Adam Smith, Adam Ferguson, and the Division of Labour", in *Economica*, vol. 35, pp. 249–259.
Hamowy R. (1987), *The Scottish Enlightenment and the Theory of Spontaneous Order*, Carbondale: Southern Illinois University Press
Hayek F.A. (1949), *Individualism and Economic Order*, London: Routledge & Kegan Paul.
Hayek F.A. (1960), *The Constitution of Liberty*, London: Routledge & Kegan Paul.
Hayek F.A. (1969), *Studies in Philosophy, Politics and Economics*, New York: Simon & Schuster.
Hayek F.A. (1978), *New Studies in Philosophy, Politics, Economics and the History of Ideas*, Chicago: University of Chicago Press.
Hayek F.A. (1979), *The Counter-Revolution of Science*, Indianapolis: Liberty Fund.
Hayek F.A. (1982), *Law, Legislation and Liberty*, London: Routledge.
Hayek F.A. (1988), *The Fatal Conceit*, London: Routledge.
Heckscher E.F. (1935), *Mercantilism*, London: Allen & Unwin.
Hesiod (A), "Works and Days", in Hesiod, *Theogony* and *Works and Days*, Oxford 1988: Oxford University Press.
Hirschman A.O. (1991), *The Rhetoric of Reaction*, Cambridge, MA: Belknap Press of Harvard University Press.
Hobbes T. ([1651] 1914), *Leviathan*, London: Dent.
Hoffmann E. (1960), *Platonismus und christliche Philosophie*, Zürich: Artemis.
Horne T.A. (1978), *The Social and Political Thought of B. Mandeville*, London: Macmillan.
Hubert R. (1923), *Les sciences sociales dans l'Encyclopédie*, Paris: Alcan.
Hubert R. (1928), *Rousseau et l'Encyclopédie*, Paris: Gamber.
Huizinga J. (1945), *Wenn die Waffen Schweigen*, Basel: Burg Verlag.
Hume D. ([1757] 1889), *The Natural History of Religion*, London: Bonner.
Hume D. ([1748] 1902a), *An Enquiry Concerning Human Understanding*, in Hume (1902c).
Hume D. ([1751] 1902b), *An Enquiry Concerning the Principles of Morals*, in Hume (1902c).
Hume D. (1902c), *Enquiries Concerning the Human Understanding and Concerning the Principles of Morals*, Oxford: Clarendon Press.
Hume D. ([1742–1757] 1903), *Essays, Moral, Political and Literary*, London: Richards.
Hume D. ([1779] 1907), *Dialogues on Natural Religion*, Edinburgh: Blackwood.
Hume D. ([1739–1740] 1930), *A Treatise of Human Nature*, London: Dent.
Hume D. ([1745] 1967), *A Letter from a Gentleman to his Friend in Edinburgh*, Edinburgh: Edinburgh University Press.
Hume D. ([1754–1761] 1983), *The History of England*, Indianapolis: Liberty Fund.
Hutcheson F. (1725a), *An Inquiry into the Original of our Ideas of Beauty and Virtue*, Dublin: Smith.
Hutcheson F. (1725b), *Reflections on the Common Systems of Morality*, in Mautner (1993).
Hutcheson F. (1730), *Inaugural Lecture on the Social Nature of Man*, in Mautner (1993).
Hutcheson F. (1750), *Reflections upon Laughter and Remarks upon The Fable of the Bees*, Glasgow: Baxter.

Hutcheson F. (1755), *A System of Moral Philosophy*, Glasgow: Foulis.
Huxley T.H. (1900), "Evolution and Ethics", in *Romanes Lectures. Decennial Issue, 1892–1900*, Oxford: Clarendon Press.
Iannello N. (1998), *L'ordine degli uomini. Antropologia e politica nel pensiero di Thomas Hobbes e di Jean-Jacques Rousseau*, Pisa and Rome: Istituti Editoriali e Poligrafici Internazionali.
Infantino L. (1998), *Individualism in Modern Thought*, London: Routledge.
Infantino L. (2003), *Ignorance and Liberty*, London: Routledge.
Infantino L. (2008), *Individualismo, mercato e storia delle idee*, Soveria Mannelli: Rubbettino.
Infantino L. (2019), *Cercatori di libertà*, Soveria Mannelli: Rubbettino.
Infantino L. (2020a), *Infrasocial Power: Political Dimensions of Human Action*, New York: Palgrave Macmillan.
Infantino L. (2020b), "Adam Smith and the Problem of Unintended Consequences", in *Journal of Public Finance and Public Choice*, vol. 35, pp. 219–236.
Israel J. (2009), *The Revolution of Mind*, Princeton: Princeton University Press.
Jaeger W. (1947), "Praise of Law", in Sayre P. (ed.), *Interpretations of Modern Legal Philosophy: Essays in Honor of Roscoe Pound*, New York: Oxford University Press.
Jaeger W. (1961), *Early Christianity and Greek Paideia*, Cambridge, MA: Harvard University Press.
Jaeger W. (1965), *Paideia: The Ideals of Greek Culture*, Oxford: Oxford University Press.
Jaffé W. (1976), "Menger, Jevons and Walras De-homogenized", in *Economic Enquiry*, vol. 14, pp. 511–524.
Jaucourt L. de (1765), *Lacédémone (Republique de)*, in *Encyclopédie*, Neufchastel: Faulche, vol. 9.
Jevons W.S. ([1871] 1888), *The Theory of Political Economy*, London: Macmillan.
Jhering R. von ([1872] 1965), *Der Kampf ums Recht*, Nürnberg: Glock & Lutz.
Kauder E. (1965), *A History of Marginal Utility Theory*, Princeton: Princeton University Press.
Kaye F.B. (1924), *Introduction*, in Mandeville ([1714–1729] 1924).
Kettler D. (1965), *The Social and Political Thought of Adam Ferguson*, Columbus: Ohio State University Press.
Keynes J.M. (1936), *The General Theory of Employment, Interest and Money*, London: Macmillan.
King-Hele D. (1985), "Erasmus Darwin: Master of Interdisciplinary Science", in *Interdisciplinary Science Review*, vol. 10, pp. 170–191.
Kirzner I.M. (1992), *The Meaning of Market Process: Essays in the Development of Modern Austrian Economics*, London: Routledge.
La Vergata A. (2005), *Guerra e darwinismo sociale*, Soveria Mannelli: Rubbettino.
Leechman W. (1755), *Preface* to Hutcheson (1755).
Lenci M. (2005), *Montesquieu, Burke e l'Illuminismo*, in Felice (2005).
Locke J. ([1690] 1924), *Essay Concerning Human Understanding*, Oxford: Clarendon Press.
Lunaciarskij A. (1973), *Religija i socializm*, Italian translation, Bologna: Guaraldi.
Machiavelli N. ([1531] 1883), *Discourses on the First Decade of Titus Livius*, London: Kegan Paul.
Magri T. (1987), *Introduzione* to B. de Mandeville, *La favola delle api*, Rome and Bari: Laterza.

Malinowski B. (1926), *Crime and Custom in Savage Society*, New York: Harcourt, Brace & Co.
Malinowski B. (1948), *Magic, Science and Religion*, Glencoe: Free Press.
Mandeville B. de (1723), *Free Thoughts on Religion, the Church and National Happiness*, London: Brotherton.
Mandeville B. de (1732), *An Enquiry into the Origin of Honour and the Usefulness of Christianity in War*, London: Brotherton.
Mandeville B. de ([1714–1729] 1924), *The Fable of the Bees*, Oxford: Clarendon Press.
Marx K. ([1867] 1976), *Capital*, London: Penguin.
Mautner T. (ed.) (1993), "Introduction" to *Francis Hutcheson: Two Texts on Human Nature*, Cambridge: Cambridge University Press.
McCosh J. (1875), *The Scottish Philosophy*, New York: Carter.
Meek D.L. (1976), *Social Science and the Ignoble Savage*, Cambridge: Cambridge University Press.
Meldola R. (1910), *Evolution: Darwinian and Spencerian*, Oxford: Clarendon Press.
Menger C. ([1871] 1994), *Principles of Economics*, Grove City: Libertarian Press.
Menger C. ([1883] 1996), *Investigations into the Method of the Social Sciences*, Grove City: Libertarian Press.
Menger C. ([1892] 2002), "Money", in Latzer M. and Schmitz S.W. (eds), *Carl Menger and the Evolution of Payments Systems*, Cheltenham, UK and Northampton, MA, USA: Edward Elgar Publishing.
Menger C. ([1891] 2016), "The Social Theories of Classical Political Economy and Modern Economic Policy", in *Econ Journal Watch*, vol. 13, pp. 473–488.
Mercier de la Rivière P.-P ([1767] 1846), "L'ordre naturel et essentiel des sociétés politique", in Daire M.E. (ed.), *Physiocrates*, vol. 2, Paris: Guillaumin.
Merton R.K. (1936), "The Unanticipated Consequences of Purposive Social Action", in *American Sociological Review*, vol. 1, pp. 894–903.
Merton R.K. (1968), *Social Theory and Social Structure*, New York: Free Press.
Meyer E. (1895), *Die wirtschaftliche Entwicklung des Altertums*, Jena: Fischer.
Mill J.S. ([1843] 1892), *A System of Logic Ratiocinative and Inductive*, London: Routledge.
Mill J.S. ([1848] 1965), *Principles of Political Economy*, Toronto: Toronto University Press.
Mill J.S. ([1844] 1967), "Essays on Some Unsettled Questions of Political Economy", in *Essays in Economics and Society*, Toronto: Toronto University Press.
Millar J. (1803), *An Historical View of the English Government*, London: Mawman.
Mises L. von (1978), *Notes and Recollections*, South Holland: Libertarian Press.
Mises L. von ([1933] 1981a), *Epistemological Problems of Economics*, New York: New York University Press.
Mises L. von ([1922] 1981b), *Socialism: An Economic and Sociological Analysis*, Indianapolis: Liberty Fund.
Mongardini C. (1970), *L'epoca della società*, Rome: Bulzoni.
Montaigne M. de ([1580] 1838), *Essais*, Paris: Didot.
Montalenti G. (1990), *Introduzione* to Darwin C., *L'origine delle specie*, Torino: Boringhieri.
Montalenti G. (2009), *Introduzione* to Darwin C., *L'origine dell'uomo e la selezion sessuale*, Rome: Newton Compton.
Montesquieu C.-L. de ([1721] 1875–79a), *Lettres persanes*, in Montesquieu (1875–79g), vol.1.

Montesquieu C.-L. de ([1725] 1875–79b), *Traité général de devoirs del'homme*, in Montesquieu (1875–79g), vol. 7.
Montesquieu C.-L. de ([1734] 1875–79c), *Considerations sur les causes de la grandeur des romains et de leur Decadence*, in Montesquieu (1875–79g), vol. 2.
Montesquieu C.-L. de ([1748] 1875–79d), *L'Esprit del lois*, Part 1, in Montesquieu (1875–79g), vol. 3.
Montesquieu C.-L. de ([1748] 1875–79e), *L'Esprit des lois*, Part 2, in Montesquieu (1875–79g), vol. 4.
Montesquieu C.-L. de ([1748] 1875–79f), *Défence de L'Esprit de lois*, in Montesquieu (1875–79g), vol. 6.
Montesquieu C.-L. de (1875–79g), *Oeuvres complètes*, Paris: Garnier.
Morganti F. (2015), *Psicologia animale ed evoluzione nel secolo di Darwin*, Pisa: Edizioni ETS.
Morrow G.R. (1923), "The Significance of the Doctrine of Sympathy in Hume and Adam Smith", in *Philosophical Review*, vol. 32, pp. 60–78.
Mossner E.C. (2001), *The Life of David Hume*, Oxford: Clarendon Press.
Nietzsche F. ([1872] 1909), *The Birth of Tragedy*, London: George Allen & Unwin.
Norton D.F. (1982), *David Hume, Common-sense Moralist, Sceptical Metaphysician*, Princeton: Princeton University Press.
Ollier F. (1933), *Le mirage spartiate*, Paris: de Boccard.
Oncken A. (1902), *Geschichte der Nationalökonomie*, Leipzig: Hirschfeld.
Oncken A. (1909), "Adam Smith und Adam Ferguson", in *Zeitschrift für Socialwissenschaft*, vol. 12, part one, pp. 129–137.
Ortega y Gasset J. ([1923] 1946–83a), *El tema de nuestro tiempo*, in Ortega y Gasset (1946–83j), vol. 3.
Ortega y Gasset J. ([1941] 1946–83b), *Apuntes sobre el pensamiento*, in Ortega y Gasset (1946–83j), vol. 5.
Ortega y Gasset J. ([1960] 1946–83c), *Origen y epílogo de la filosofía*, in Ortega y Gasset (1946–83j), vol. 9.
Ortega y Gasset J. ([1948] 1946–83d), *Prospecto del Instituto de humanidades*, in Ortega y Gasset (1946–83j), vol. 7.
Ortega y Gasset J. ([1960] 1946–83e), *Una interpretación de la historia universal*, in Ortega y Gasset (1946–83j), vol. 9.
Ortega y Gasset J. ([1958] 1946–83f), *La idea de principio en Leibniz*, Ortega y Gasset (1946–83j), vol. 8.
Ortega y Gasset J. ([1930] 1946–83g), *La rebelión de las masas*, in Ortega y Gasset (1946–83j), vol. 4.
Ortega y Gasset J. ([1928] 1946–83h), *La "Filosofía de la Historia" de Hegel y la Historiología*, in Ortega y Gasset (1946–83j), vol. 4.
Ortega y Gasset, J. ([1939] 1946–83i), *Meditación de la tecnica*, in Ortega y Gasset (1946–83j), vol. 5.
Ortega y Gasset J. (1946–83j), *Obras completas*, Madrid: Revista de Occidente.
Otto R. (1926), *Das Heilige*, Gotha: Klotz.
Paganini G. (1980), *Analisi della fede e critica della ragione nella filosofia di Pierre Bayle*, Florence: La Nuova Italia.
Palmer L.R. (1950), "The Indo-European Origin of Greek Justice", in *Transactions of Philosophical Society*, vol. 49, pp. 149–168.
Paoli U.E. (1933), *Studi sul processo attico*, Padova: Cedam.
Paoli U.E. (1976), *Altri studi di diritto greco e romano*, Milan: La Goliardica.

Patten S.N. (1899), *The Development of English Thought: A Study in the Economic Interpretation of History*, New York: Macmillan.
Pellicani L. (1992), *L'individualismo metodologico. Una critica*, in Antiseri D., Pellicani L., *L'individualismo metodologico*, Milan: Angeli.
Pellicani L. (2011), *Dalla città sacra alla città secolare*, Soveria Mannelli: Rubbettino.
Plato (A), "Apology", in Plato (E).
Plato (B), "Republic", in Plato (E).
Plato (C), "Laws", in Plato (E).
Plato (D), "Lettera VII", in Plato (E).
Plato (E), *Collected Dialogues of Plato*, Princeton: Princeton University Press.
Plutarch (A), *Lives*, vol. 1, Cambridge, MA: Harvard University Press; London: Heinemann.
Pocock J.G.A. (1985), *Virtue, Commerce and History*, Cambridge: Cambridge University Press.
Pohlenz M. (1947), *Der hellenische Mensch*, Göttingen: Vandenhoeck & Ruprecht.
Pohlenz M. (1954), *Die Griechischte Tragödie*, Göttingen: Vandenhoeck & Ruprecht.
Polanyi K. (1977), *The Livelihood of Man*, New York: Academic Press.
Pollock F. Sir (1908), *Oxford Lectures and Other Essays*, London: Macmillan.
Popper K.R. (1966), *The Open Society and its Enemies*, London: Routledge.
Popper K.R. (1974), *Objective Knowledge*, Oxford: Clarendon Press.
Popper K.R. (1977), "The Self and its Brain", in Popper K.R., Eccles J.C., *The Self and its Brain*, Berlin and New York: Springer International.
Popper K.R. (1979), *Objective Knowledge: An Evolutionary Approach*, Oxford: Clarendon Press.
Popper K.R. (1991), *Conjectures and Refutations*, London: Routledge.
Popper K.R., Lorenz K. (1985), *Die Zukunft ist Offen*, Munich and Zürich: Piper.
Prior J. Sir (1891), *A Life of Edmund Burke*, London: Bell.
Protagoras (A), "Frammenti", in *I presocratici*, Rome and Bari 1999: Laterza.
Pseudo-Xenophon (A), *The Constitution of the Athenians*, London 2017: Association of Classical Teachers.
Quesnay F. ([1765] 1846), "Droit naturelle", in Daire M.E. (ed.), *Physiocrates*, vol. 1, Paris: Guillaumin.
Rae J. (1895), *Life of Adam Smith*, London: Macmillan.
Raphael D.D. (1974), *Hume's Critique of Ethical Rationalism*, in Todd W.B. (ed.), *Hume and the Enlightenment*, Edinburgh: Edinburgh University Press.
Raphael D.D., Macfie A.L. (1976), *Introduction* to Smith ([1759] 1976–83a).
Rasmussen D.C. (2017), *The Infidel and the Professor*, Princeton: Princeton University Press.
Rawson E. (1969), *The Spartan Tradition in European Thought*, Oxford: Oxford University Press.
Robertson J.M. (1900), *Introduction* to Shaftesbury ([1711] 1900).
Romilly J. de (1970), *La tragédie grecque*, Paris: PUF.
Rosenberg N. (1963), "Mandeville and Laissez-faire", in *Journal of History of Ideas*, vol. 24, pp. 183–196.
Ross I. (1966), "Hutcheson on Hume's Treatise: An Unnoticed Letter", in *Journal of the History of Philosophy*, vol. 4, pp. 69–72.
Ross I. (1987), *Foreword* to Hamowy (1987).
Rousseau J.-J. ([1762] 1974), *Emile*, London: Dent.
Rousseau J.-J. ([1750] 1997), "Discourse on the Science and Art", in *The Discourses and Other Early Political Writings*, Cambridge: Cambridge University Press.

Russell B. (1956), *Portraits from Memory*, London: Allen & Unwin.
Salomon A. (1945), "Adam Smith as Sociologist", in *Social Research*, vol. 12, pp. 22–42.
Savigny F. von (1816), "Stimmen für und wider neue Gesetzbücher", in *Zeitschrift für geschichtliche Rechtswissenschaft*, vol. 3, pp. 1–52.
Schatz A. (1907), *L'individualisme économique et social*, Paris: Colin.
Scheler M. (1923), "Zum Phänomen des Tragischen", in *Vom Umsturz der Werte, Der Abhandlungen und Aufsätze zweite Durchgesehene Auflage*, Leipzig: Der Neue Geist-Verlag.
Schultz G. (1969), *Das Zeitalter der Gesellschaft*, Munich: Piper.
Schumpeter J.A. (1908), *Das Wesen und der Hauptinhalt der theoritischen Nationalökonomie*, Munich and Leipzig: Duncker & Humblot.
Schumpeter J.A. (1914), "Epochen der Dogmen-und Methodengeschichte", in *Grundriss der Socialökonomik*, vol. 1, Tübingen: Mohr.
Schumpeter J.A. (1954), *History of Economic Analysis*, New York: Oxford University Press.
Scott W.R. (1900), *Francis Hutcheson*, Cambridge: Cambridge University Press.
Scott W.R. (1937), *Adam Smith as Student and Professor*, Glasgow: Jackson.
Scribano M.E. (1980), *Natura umana e società competitiva*, Milan: Feltrinelli.
Sebastiani S. (2005), *L'Esprit des lois nel discorso storico dell'Illuminismo scozzese*, in Felice (2005), vol. 1.
Sen A. (1987), *On Ethics and Economics*, Oxford: Blackwell.
Shaftesbury Lord ([1711] 1900), *Characteristics*, London: Richards.
Simmel G. (1908), *Soziologie*, Leipzig: Duncker & Humblot.
Simmel G. (1910), *Hautprobleme der Philosophie*, Leipzig: Göschen Verlashandlung.
Simmel G. ([1900] 1978), *The Philosophy of Money*, London: Routledge & Kegan Paul.
Simonazzi M. (2015), *Le favole della filosofia. Saggio su Bernard de Mandeville*, Milan: Angeli.
Small A. (1907), *Adam Smith and Modern Sociology*, Chicago: University of Chicago Press.
Smith A. ([1759] 1976–83a), *The Theory of Moral Sentiments*, in Smith (1976–83f).
Smith A. ([1776] 1976–83b), *An Inquiry into the Causes of the Wealth of Nations*, in Smith (1976–83f).
Smith A. ([1795] 1976–83c), *Essays on Philosophical Subjects*, in Smith (1976–83f).
Smith A. ([1962–1764] 1976–83d), *Lectures on Jurisprudence*, in Smith (1976–83f).
Smith A. ([1740–1790] 1976–83e), *Correspondence*, in Smith (1976–83f).
Smith A. (1976–83f), *Works and Correspondence*, Oxford: Clarendon Press.
Sombart W. (1923), "Die Anfänge der Soziologie", in *Hautprobleme der Soziologie: Erinnerrungsgabe für Max Weber*, Munich and Leipzig: Duncker & Humbolt.
Sombart W. [1934] 1937), *A New Social Philosophy*, Princeton: Princeton University Press.
Spencer H. (1852), "A Theory of Population, deduced from the General Law of Animal Fertility", in *Westminster Review*, vol. 9, pp. 1–35.
Spencer H. (1857), "Progress: Its Law and Cause", in *Westminster Review*, vol. 11, pp. 431–485.
Spencer H. (1860), "The Social Organism", in *Westminster Review*, vol. 17, pp. 90–132.
Spencer H. (1873), *The Study of Sociology*, London: King.
Spencer H. ([1864] 1886), *The Principles of Biology*, New York: Appleton.
Spencer H. ([1862] 1887), *First Principles*, London: Williams & Norgate.

Spencer H. (1891), *Essays: Scientific, Political and Speculative*, London: Williams & Norgate.
Spencer H. (1904), *Autobiography*, London: Williams & Norgate.
Spencer H. ([1877–1896] 1906), *The Principles of Sociology*, New York: Appleton.
Spencer H. ([1879] 1907), *The Data of Ethics*, London: Williams & Norgate.
Spencer H. ([1884] 1978), *The Principles of Ethics*, Indianapolis: Liberty Fund.
Spencer H. ([1851] 1995), *Social Statics*, New York: Schalkenbach Foundation.
Stephen L. (1902), *History of English Thought in the Eighteenth Century*, London: Murray.
Stewart D. (1829), *Dissertation Exhibiting a General View of the Progress of Metaphysical, Ethical and Political Philosophy, Since the Revival of Letters in Europe*, Cambridge: Hilliard & Brown.
Stewart D. ([1828] 1859), *The Philosophy of the Active and Moral Power of Man*, Boston: Phillips & Sampson.
Stewart D. ([1793] 1980), *Account of the Life and Writings of Adam Smith*, in Smith (1976–83c).
Strauss L. (1965), *Natural Right and History*, Chicago: University of Chicago Press.
Swift J. ([1708] 2004), *An Argument against Abolishing Christianity*, Adelaide: eBooks.
Tarde G. (1895), *La logique sociale*, Paris: Alcan.
Thiébault D. (1860), *Souvenirs de vingt ans de séjour à Berlin*, Paris: Didot.
Thucydides (A), *The Peloponnesian War*, Oxford 1966: Sadler & Brown.
Tocqueville A. de (1856), *The Old Regime and the French Revolution*, New York: Harper.
Tocqueville A. de ([1835–1840] 1994), *Democracy in America*, London: Everyman's Library.
Trevor-Roper H. (1967), "The Scottish Enlightenment", in *Studies on Voltaire and the Eighteenth Century*, vol. 58, pp. 1635–1658.
Tucker J. (1755), *The Elements of Commerce, and Theory of Taxes*, Bristol.
Turco L. (2005), *Hume e Montesquieu*, in Felice (2005), vol. 1.
Tylor E.B. (1903), *Primitive Culture*, London: Murray.
Viner J. (1927), "Adam Smith and Laissez Faire", in *Journal of Political Economy*, vol. 35, pp. 198–232.
Viner J. (1937), *Studies in the Theory of International Trade*, London: Allen & Unwin.
Viner J. (1958), *The Long View and the Short*, Glencoe: Free Press.
Voltaire ([1752] 1822), *Dictionnaire philosophique*, Paris: Jouquet.
Vorzimmer P.J. (1972), *Charles Darwin: The Years of Controversy*, London: University of London Press.
Walras L. (1896), *Études d'économie sociale*, Lausanne: Rougé.
Weber M. (1924), *Gesammelte Aufsätze zur Sozial- und Wirtschaftsgeschichte*, Tübingen: Mohr.
Weber M. ([1917] 1949), "The Meaning of 'Ethical Neutrality' in Sociology and Economics", in *On the Methodology of Social Sciences*, Glencoe: Free Press.
Weber M. ([1919] 1970a), "Politics as a Vocation", in Weber (1970c).
Weber M. ([1919] 1970b) "Science as a Vocation", in Weber (1970c)
Weber M. (1970c), *Essays in Sociology*, London: Routledge.
Weber M. ([1922] 1978), *Economy and Society*, Berkeley: University of California Press.
White L.A. (1949), *The Science of Culture*, New York: Farrar, Straus & Co.
Wolin S.S. (2006), *Politics and Vision*, Princeton: Princeton University Press.

Wood D. (1986), "Constant in Edinburgh: Eloquence and History", in *French Studies*, vol. 40, pp. 151–166.

Xenophon (A), "Memorabilia", in *Memorabilia and Oeconomicus*, London and New York 1923: Heinemann/Putnam.

Zemek T. (1987), "Benjamin Constant, Adam Smith and the 'moule universel': The Impartial Spectator and his 'Social Framework", in *Annales Benjamin Constant*, vol. 7, pp. 49–63.

Index

abstract order 7, 81
alteration 70, 72
Anaxagoras 14
anti-individualism 32
antipathy 82
Aristotle 1, 4, 14, 79
atheism 23, 35, 60
Augustine of Hippo 10
autonomy 6, 7, 15, 47, 63, 81

Bacon, F. 19–20, 32, 36
Bartley, W.W. III 32
Bayle, P. x, 19, 21–4, 25, 28, 29, 32, 33, 42
Bel, J.-J. 58
benevolence 40, 50, 52, 56, 57, 68
Bentham, J. xi, 49–50, 75, 82–4, 94–5
Bernier, F. 57
Biscardi, A. 15
Black, J. 74
Blair, H. 69
Bobbio, N. 32
Boudon, R. 104
Burckhardt, J. 8
Burke, E. 56, 78–82, 85–6, 92, 93, 97

Carmichael, G. 39, 51
Catherine of Russia 37
Cato the Censor 34
causation theory 53
Chardin, J. 57
Charicles 15
choice x, xi, 7, 96
    individual freedom of 6, 15, 20, 27, 33, 47–9, 59, 62–3, 67, 81, 94
    personal 23, 25, 45
Cicero 34, 44
co-adaptation 28, 39, 47, 49, 65, 67, 78–9, 89, 90
compatibility of actions 41

composition 6, 7, 21
compositive method xi, xii, 85
compulsory cogency 10
Comte, A. 17, 56, 86–9, 96
Condorcet, A.-N. de 86–7
consciousness 20, 64, 89
consequences, paradox of 41, 49
Constant, B. 14, 73, 78–82, 93, 94
continuities and discontinuities 78–98
    Burke and Constant (Scottish influences) 78–82
    Comte (discontinuity) and Spencer (continuity) 86–9
    Spencer and Darwin 90–92
    utilitarianism in broad sense and narrow sense 82–6
contractualist theories 11
cooperation x, 49, 54
    Burke and Constant 81
    coercive 62, 67, 73
    Hume and unintended order 46–7
    internal 36
    Tucker 50
    with unknown persons 103
    utilitarianism in narrow sense and broad sense 83
    voluntary 7, 30, 50, 62, 67, 73, 102
    see also social cooperation
Coser, L. 97
culture and religion, split between 5
Cumberland, R. 41

Darwin, C. ix–x, 55–6, 84, 90–92, 97, 98, 99–100, 103, 104
Darwin, E. 90
Darwinism 98
    see also social Darwinism
Dawkins, R. 34
Dennett, D.C. 97
Descartes, R. 17, 19–21, 94

development hypothesis 91, 98
Diderot, D. 72
Dilthey, W. 16–17
divine powers 1, 2, 4, 21
divine will ix, 3, 4, 11, 13, 21, 49, 72
divinity 2, 4, 11, 12, 39, 41, 44
division of labour 35, 36, 62, 66–8, 75, 77, 96, 97
    Comte and Spencer 89
    Hume and unintended order 46
    Spencer and Darwin 90
Dunn, W.C. 93
Durkheim, É. 11, 17, 75

economic values 86
Ehrenberg, V. 14
Ehrlich, E. 95
Epicurus 52, 73
Erasmus 24, 32, 34, 55
errors, correction of 49, 102
ethical paradoxes 4, 13
Euripides tragedies 5, 13
evolutionism 49, 82, 85, 90–91, 98, 102
    cultural xi, 30, 101, 103

faith 1, 5, 7, 8, 21
    religious 2, 4, 23
fallibility 57
    and unintended order 24–8
    see also ignorance and fallibility
false religions 22
Ferguson, A. 48, 69–70, 76, 77, 80
Filangieri, G. 93
final causes 45
Fontana, B. 93
Frazer, J.G. 1, 12
French Enlightenment 72
French positivism 94
French rationalism 30
Friedrich, C.J. 16
Fustel de Coulanges, N.-D. 1, 12

Galileo 21
government of the law xi, 6–7, 47–8
government of men xi, 6–7, 47
gravitation principle 40
Great Legislator 3, 6, 11, 17, 20, 47, 85, 87

great and most extensive happiness 49–50
Greek tragedy 1, 4
Grote, G. 8
Guizot, F. 13, 94
Guyau, J.M. 94

Halévy, É. 38, 56, 84, 94
Hamilton, Sir W. 39
Harrington, J. 73
Hayek, F.A. von 18, 32, 33, 36, 53, 55, 75, 95, 96, 103
    individualism, true and false 20–21
    Mandeville: human fallibility and unintended order 28
    utilitarianism in narrow sense and broad sense 85–6
Heckscher, E.F. 29, 36
Hegel, G.W.F. 17
Hesiod 104
heteronomy 15
Hirschman, A.O. 103, 104
historical-social context 57
Hitler, A. 17
Hobbes, T. 29, 32, 36, 39, 40, 42
Holbach, P.-H. d' 72
Home, H. (later Lord Kames) 42, 50, 53, 56
honour 1, 52, 61
Hooker, J.D. 91
human perfectibility 87
humanization and social relationships 65
Hume, D. ix–x, xi, 1, 30–31, 36, 38, 52–3, 55–6, 70, 71, 74, 77
    betrayed by Hutcheson 42–5
    between past and future 39
    Burke and Constant 78
    Ferguson 69–70
    Montesquieu and myth of Sparta and the Great Society 62
    Montesquieu and variability of models of life 59
    polytheism 3–4
    research traditions 49
    Smith, division of labour and rule of law 68
    Smith and social norms 63–4, 65
    Spencer and Darwin 90
    Tucker 50–51
    and unintended order 45–8

utilitarianism in narrow sense and
    broad sense 85
Hutcheson, F. x, 38, 39–42, 48–50, 51,
    52, 53, 76
  betrayal of Hume 42–5
  Hume and unintended order 45
  Smith, division of labour and rule of
    law 68
Hutton, J. 74
Huxley, T.H. 100, 101, 102, 104

Ibben 57–8
ideal society 8
ignorance and fallibility 20, 21, 25, 49,
    102
  Burke and Constant 79–81
  Comte and Spencer 88
  Hume and unintended order 45–6
  Mandeville: human fallibility and
    unintended order 27
  Smith, division of labour and rule of
    law 68
  utilitarianism in narrow sense and
    broad sense 84
individual and collective life 31, 39
individual interest 85
individualism 29, 32
  methodological xi, 85
  true and false 19–21
innocent guilt 4
intended outcomes 1, 2, 7
intentional actions 6
intentional order 6, 7–10, 23, 27, 30–31,
    33, 48, 49, 60, 68, 84
intentions, controlling 3
intersubjective interaction 99
invisible hand 63, 66, 67

Jaeger, W. 6, 13, 14, 15
Jaucourt, L. de 61–2
Jevons, W.S. 84

Kames, Lord 42, 50, 53, 56
Kant, I. 17
Kaye, F.B. 24, 29–30, 33, 34, 44
Keynes, J.M. 36
Kirzner, I.M. 96
knowledge of time and place 57, 75

La Mothe le Vayer, F. de 33
labour theory of value 86
Laconomania 61
laissez-faire 30–31
Lamarckism 98
Lankester, E.R. 91
Le Sage, G.-L. 70
Leechman, W. 44
Lenci, M. 73
liberals 28–31
Locke, J. 43
Lorenz, K. 74
Lucretius 44, 52
Lycurgus 37, 62

Mably, G.B. de 72
McCosh, J. 38–9
Macfie, A.L. 76
Machiavelli, N. 73
Mackintosh, Sir J. 90, 97
magic 1–2, 13, 15
Magri, T. 36
Malinowski, B. 1, 13, 15
Malthus, T.R. 90, 97
Mandeville, B. de ix–x, 19, 28–31, 34,
    35, 36, 37, 49, 52, 53, 56, 70
  between past and future 38–9
  human fallibility and unintended
    order 24–8
  Hume betrayed by Hutcheson 44
  Hume and unintended order 46
  Hutcheson 40, 41–2
  Montesquieu and myth of Sparta
    and the Great Society 62
  Montesquieu and variability of
    models of life 59
  Smith, division of labour and rule of
    law 68
  utilitarianism in narrow sense and
    broad sense 86
manifest truth 19–20, 22–3, 30
Marx, K. 17, 35
mediation 30
Meek, D.L. 77
Meldola, R. 98, 99, 100
Menger, C. xi, xii, 84–6, 95, 96
mercantilists 28–31
Mercier de la Rivière, P.-P. 37
Merton, R.K. 12, 92
metaphysical stage (humanity) 87

Meyer, E. 7
Mill, J.S. 83–4
Millar, J. 48, 76
Minos 37, 62
mirror metaphor 64
Mises, L. von 35, 96
Molesworth, R. 51
monarchical government 61
monotheism 10
Montagu, E. 69–70
Montaigne, M. de 24, 32, 33
Montalenti, G. 104
Montesquieu, C.-L. de ix, xi, 56, 70, 71, 72, 73, 77, 93
  Comte and Spencer 86–7
  myth of Sparta and the Great Society 60–63
  variability of models of life 57–9
morality 24, 38, 43, 45, 65, 89
Morellet, A. 30, 37
Mossner, E.C. 44
mutual benefit 34, 89
mythological fantasies 6

natural law 11
natural selection 91–2, 98, 99, 100, 102
negative character of outcomes 3, 7, 12, 21, 27, 48, 49, 103
negative effects generating positive results 41
neo-classical economics 84
Newton, I. 63
Nicholas of Cusa 32
Nietzsche, F. 5, 13
normative habitat xi, 67

obligations, fulfilment of 47
omniscience 11, 21, 79, 88
Oncken, A. 37, 77
optimistic epistemology 20
'original Mind' or 'original being' 41
Ortega y Gasset, J. xii, 5, 6, 12, 13, 14, 17, 37, 75

Paganini, G. 33
Patten, S.N. 103
Pellicani, L. 32
Pericles 6, 73
peripeteia 4

personal motivation and social justification action 25, 27
Peuchet, J. 37
Plato 7–10, 14, 15–16, 17, 37, 62, 71
Pocock, J.G.A. 71
Pohlenz, M. 4, 14
politics and religion, separation between 25
Pollock, Sir F. 56
polytheism 2–6, 63
Popper, K.A. 15, 17, 18, 32, 75, 98, 104
  Comte and Spencer 88
  government of men and government of the law 7
  individualism, true and false 19–21
  Plato and new intentional order 10
  polytheism 2–3
  Smith and social norms 64
positive character of outcomes x, 3, 7, 12, 48
positive effects generating negative results 41
positive law 38
positive stage (humanity) 87–8
profane 1, 2, 6, 21, 25
Protagoras 5, 7
Pseudo-Xenophon (Critias) 14, 15, 16
psychomorphism 13
public benefits 29
public good 40, 46, 61
purgation 9
purposive social action 12

Quesnay, F. 30–31, 37

radical conflict of principle 1
Raphael, D.D. 76
Rasmussen, D.C. 74
rationalism
  Cartesian 21
  ethical 43
  French 30
Rawson, E. 61, 63
reactionary theories 7, 32, 103
reciprocity 15, 86
regulatory habitat 81
religion and magic 1–2
religious belief 6, 8, 13, 25, 42, 43, 45

and superstitious belief,
    intermingling of 22
research traditions 48–50
Rhedi 59
Rica 57–8
ritual 1, 2
Robertson, W. 48, 69
Rochefoucauld, F. de la 24
Rousseau, J.-J. 61, 72
rule of justice 81
rule of law 27, 49, 66–8, 101
    Burke and Constant 80, 82
    Hume and unintended order 47
    Montesquieu and myth of Sparta
        and the Great Society 61–2
    utilitarianism in narrow sense and
        broad sense 84
rule of men 68, 80, 84
rules and institutions 3, 30, 49, 57, 89, 99
Russell, B. 83–4
Rycaut, P. 57

sacred 1, 4, 13, 21
Saint-Simon, H. de 17
Salomon, A. 20, 65
Savigny, F. von 56, 85, 95
scarcity ix, 8, 26, 45–6, 54, 82, 83
Schatz, A. 29–30, 35
Scheler, M. 1, 7–10, 16
Schumpeter, J. xi, 31, 37, 74, 77, 84
Scott, W.R. 43–4
Scottish Enlightenment xi, 39, 80, 102
selection 104
    see also natural selection
self-love 50, 51, 68
Sen, A. 76
Shaftesbury, Lord 29, 39–42, 51, 52
Sidney, A. 73
Simmel, G. 75, 102
Small, A. 96
Smith, A. ix, xi, 12, 29, 35, 36, 56, 57,
    74, 75, 76, 77, 92, 93, 95, 97, 103
    Burke and Constant 78–80, 82
    Comte and Spencer 87, 89
    division of labour and rule of law
        66–8
    Ferguson 69–70
    Mandeville: human fallibility and
        unintended order 27, 28
    research traditions 48

social norms 63–6
Spencer and Darwin 90
utilitarianism in narrow sense and
    broad sense 85–6
social approval 35
social cooperation 99, 101
    Burke and Constant 79
    Comte and Spencer 89
    Hutcheson 41
    Mandeville: human fallibility and
        unintended order 26
    Montesquieu and myth of Sparta
        and the Great Society 62
    Montesquieu and variability of
        models of life 59
    Smith and social norms 66
social Darwinism 100, 102, 103, 104
social interactions 26, 57, 65, 70, 83
social justification 23, 25, 26, 27, 33,
    60, 62
social norms 28, 63–6, 78, 79, 99
social order 3, 12, 21, 24, 29, 32, 50, 56
    between past and future 38–9
    Ferguson 69
    Hume and unintended order 45
    Hutcheson 42
social phenomena ix, xi, xii, 1, 18, 49,
    58, 64, 78, 85, 86, 88, 96
    Smith 64, 76, 78
    Spencer 92, 97, 99
social rules 11, 79, 89
social values 86
Socrates 7, 15, 20, 22
Socratic doubt 21
Solon 63
Sombart, W. 11, 17
Sophocles 4
sovereignty 30, 58, 87, 88, 93, 95
Sparta 7–8, 20, 63, 69, 70, 72, 77
    and the Great Society 60–63
Spencer, H. x, 1, 73, 90–92, 95, 96, 97,
    98, 99, 102
    continuity 86–9
    utilitarianism in narrow sense and
        broad sense 83
Stephen, L. 38, 41
Stewart, D. xi, 78, 80, 90, 101
Stoics 73
Strauss, L. 32
Swift, J. 33

sympathy 65, 74, 78, 82, 83, 89, 90, 97, 104

Tavernier, J.-B. 57
theological stage (humanity) 87
Tocqueville, A. de 31, 37, 94
totalitarianism 7, 10, 16, 33, 72
Trevor-Roper, H. 39, 48–9
trial and error 27, 81, 98
Tucker, J. 50–51, 56
Turgot, A.-R.-J. 17, 56, 87
Tylor, E.B. 13

unconditional historical prophecy 88
unknown, exploration of 102
unlimited freedom of conscience 87
Usbek 58, 59, 70, 71
utilitarianism xi, 48–9, 56, 82–6, 94, 96
utility of rules 47, 49, 82

variability of models of life 57
veracitas dei 19
veracitas naturae 19
vices, private 29
Viner, J. 29–30, 36, 76
virtue 9, 27–8, 40, 42–5, 50, 52, 58, 60–62, 67, 73, 76, 95
Voltaire 32, 72
von Boehm-Bawerk, E. 86
von Wieser, F. 86

Wallace, A.R. 91
Walras, L. 84–5, 95
Weber, M. ix, 12, 35, 86, 97, 103
White, L.A. 101, 103
wisdom, latent 79
Wishart, Rev. W. 53

Zemek, T. 80